David Watson

How to Find God

*"You will find me
when you seek me"
Jeremiah 29:13*

Harold Shaw Publishers
Wheaton, Illinois

photography:
Daniel D. Miller

Unless otherwise indicated
all Scripture quotations are from
the Revised Standard Version.

Harold Shaw Publishers edition 1976
published by special arrangement
with Falcon Books, London.

ISBN 0-87788-309-4
Library of Congress catalog card number
76-43125

First printing, September 1976

Printed in the United States of America

Contents

INTRODUCTION

Some years ago a nation wide radio network produced a program describing six major religions of the world, including Christianity. They looked for a title which would serve as a common denominator for all six religions. They called the program *Man in search of God.*

This was a very fair description of man's search for spiritual reality, which is to be found all over the world, from pagan ritual to cathedral worship, from ouija board experiments to pentecostal fervor, from radical theology to biblical authority, from transcendental meditation to missionary outreach. In countless ways, we see this search for God, or at least for some kind of spiritual reality. *Is* there anything which transcends the material world of the five senses? *Is* there a power or person greater than ourselves able to lift us out of our meaningless existence up to what is real and true?

And if there is no God, if God is dead, if there are no knowable answers, what then? Many today realize the total futility of life unless there is some infinite yet definite reference point. Naturally, therefore, even in the most sophisticated scientific or philosophical circles, we find man in search of God.

In some respects, this is not such a good title for the Christian faith. The prophets of the Old Testament, the apostles of the New, and supremely Jesus himself, were all insistent on one point: that *God is in search of man.* "For the Son of man came to seek and save the lost," said Jesus to one bewildered man, startled by the discovery that God had taken the initiative in the search. This is the Christian contention, that God has made and always makes, the first move.

Nevertheless, we are not to be passive observers. And if the Christian revelation stresses God's initiative, it calls equally for our response. "You will seek me and find me; when you seek me with all your heart, *I will be found by you,*" said God through the prophet Jeremiah. Jesus said the same thing, "Seek, and *you will find.*" It would seem that the meeting-point occurs when God's search for man and man's search for God coincide.

This is what this book is all about. In our search for God, where do we start? What assurance can we have that there is a God to be found at all? Has he spoken to us? Has he shown himself? Where can we find him? How can we find him? How shall we know if and when we have found him? What relevance has all this for today?

The substance of these chapters has come from material presented at a number of university missions during the last two or three years. Not only at these universities, but in many towns and cities in different parts of the world, it has been increasingly obvious to me that the vast majority of men, women and young people, from widely different backgrounds and cultures, are searching for God.

8

I am deeply grateful for all that I have learned from those who have helped me on these missions, and from Christian students who have frequently shown me the reality of God in their own lives.

My gratitude, too, must be expressed to Miss Mary Pratt, my tireless and patient secretary, and to the publications department of the Church Pastoral Aid Society which has encouraged and guided me in the writing of this book.

1
WHY ONLY JESUS?

No one can dispute the intense interest in the person of Jesus today. Admittedly the established churches are not heading the opinion polls for popularity. Nevertheless the focus of attention all over the world has been swinging back to Jesus Christ.

The musicals *Godspell* and *Jesus Christ Superstar* have scored hits in the world of entertainment. Jesus Festivals and Jesus Marches have attracted tens of thousands. Jesus movements have left their mark on countless young people who were previously far removed from conventional church-going. Christian groups and Fellowships which center unashamedly on the person of Jesus are booming. Recent student missions in Oxford and Cambridge have seen an average of almost 1,000 students each night for eight nights in a row at the main meetings. The subject? *Jesus Christ Today, Christ Alive.* What other society, or what other theme, could draw such numbers?

The Bible, too, continues to be the world's best seller. For example, the complete Living Bible (a modern paraphrase) sold twelve million copies in two years, and is currently selling at the rate of *ten thousand copies a day!* To say nothing of the sales of the New Testament alone, or other sections of the Bible! And this is only one version! Why such astonishing popularity? Because the substance of the Bible is still utterly compelling; and the heart of that substance is Jesus Christ.

Every now and then you will find this advertisement in the newspapers: "Born in poverty. Lived only 33 years. Spent most of his life in obscurity. Never wrote a book. Never had any position in public life. Was crucified with two thieves. And yet, 2,000 years later, more than 950 million people follow him." Although that figure no doubt includes many who are purely nominal Christians the final comment from the advertisers seems justified: "Surely it must be worthwhile to find out more about Christ."

Why Jesus?

Why do we start with him? Why not with God himself? Or why not go further back still and consider some of the philosophical questions that lie behind the whole assumption of God's existence?

When Paul visited Corinth, he found there two distinct groups in that multi-racial and permissive society; and the situation in this respect, at least, has changed very little in 2,000 years.

First, there were those who demanded tangible proof. "If God is God," they said, "let him prove himself. Let him do something. Let him demonstrate to us his existence."

The agnostic writer James Mitchell once wrote: "The value of a god must be open to test. No god is worth preserving unless he is of some practical use in

11

curing the ills which plague humanity—all the disease and pain and starvation, the little children born crippled or spastic or mentally defective: a creator god would be answerable to *us* for these things at the day of judgement—if he dared to turn up."[1] In other words, we want a satisfying sign, some tangible proof that God exists, especially in the meaningless and shockingly cruel muddle of the world today.

Second, Paul found those who were always asking questions: searching, seeking, discussing, debating, submitting all religious concepts to human reason. So it is today. "First of all," wrote Stephen Hopkinson, "I want a god who makes sense out of life as we know it, who gives meaning to the natural processes of the universe. Second, I want a god who makes sense of the existence of 'me', the personality of which I am conscious in myself...."[2] I want a god I can understand, who fits in with my rational thought, and who answers some of my deepest questions.

What did Paul say to both those groups, the one requiring a sign, the other seeking after wisdom? "We preach Christ crucified!" he said. This may be a stumbling block to some and stupid to others, but Christ in fact is both the wisdom and the power of God. Therefore if we want to understand God, we must start with Jesus. If we want to experience the power and reality of God, we must begin with Jesus.

Jesus himself once said exactly the same thing. His disciples were asking some basic questions: What is the way to God? What is God like? They were puzzled and confused, as are many today. Do you really want to know the way to God, asked Jesus: "I am the way, I am the truth, I am the life; no one goes to the Father except by me."[3] Do you really want to see God? "Whoever has seen me has seen the Father."[4]

Of course, if there is an infinite personal God at all, then by definition he is infinitely greater than our total finite human understanding. Therefore we could not begin to understand him unless he had revealed himself to us. Man by wisdom cannot find God, said Paul, and this surely is obvious: the greatest philosophers in the world have discussed the question of God's existence for 3,000 years, with no final answers to their questions at all! Most have now given up the search, and narrow the field to linguistic analysis instead!

God must therefore be known by revelation. He must "speak" to us in ways which we can understand. Otherwise, no communication is possible. The urgent question therefore is this: Is there any word from God? Has he spoken to us?

The biblical answer is quite clear: "In the past God spoke to our ancestors many times and in many ways through the prophets, but in these last days he has spoken to us through his Son."[5] "Before the world was created, the Word already existed, he was with God, and he was the same as God. . . . The Word became a human being and lived among us. We saw his glory, full of grace and truth. This was the glory which he received as the Father's only Son."[6] Devastating claims! Here is God communicating himself in the most meaningful way possible to human beings: not in a philosophy, nor in a metaphysical or ethical system; but "the Word became a human being." Here is something we can really understand. It communicates with people of all races of all generations, irrespective of culture, creed, education, environment. We are not discussing

13

some "eternal consciousness," some "impersonal life-force" or "cosmic energy" (whatever those words mean). This is the most tangible self-revelation of God anyone could possibly ask for—the Word became a human being!

Martin Luther once said about Jesus: "He ate, drank, slept, waked; was weary, sorrowful, rejoicing; he wept and he laughed; he knew hunger and thirst and sweat; he talked, he toiled, he prayed . . . so that there was no difference between him and other men, save only this, that he was God and had no sin." Now the God who has revealed himself like that is someone whom we can understand. He communicates. Some were hit by the message of Jesus so powerfully that they tried desperately to destroy him. They were unable to escape the challenge that God's Son conveyed.

"Show us the Father, and we shall be satisfied," others responded hungrily: But there was no further answer needed when Jesus replied, "Whoever has seen me has seen the Father." That is why we must start with the person of Jesus in our search for God. But . . .

Why only Jesus?
This is the stumbling block of today: the uniqueness and exclusiveness of Christ—that he claims to be the only way to God and to heaven and to life. Believe in God himself, if you want to; seek after religious experiences, follow one guru or another—but why only Jesus?

Jesus Christ Superstar,
Who do you think that they say you are?
Most people believe that the different religions of

14

world are like different paths up a mountain, all leading to the top. Which track you take is of no great importance. Whether or not there is anything at the top of the mountain may be a matter for debate. But the common view is that Christianity is simply one of the great religions of the world, and that Christ is simply one of the great religious teachers—not the only one.

Gandhi once said, "The need of the moment is not one religion but mutual respect and tolerance of the different religions. . . . The soul of religions is one, but it is encased in a multitude of forms. Truth is the exclusive property of no single scripture. . . . I cannot ascribe exclusive divinity to Jesus. He is as divine as Krishna or Rama or Mohammed or Zoroaster."[7]

A song by Quintessence says over and over again, "Jesus, Buddha, Moses, Gauranga; Jesus, Buddha, Moses, Gauranga." This is the spirit of the age. The all-embracing religion is Love. Although the Bible says "God is love," most people today read that the other way round: "Love is God." Providing you love, that is a manifestation of God; and it does not matter at all what you believe or which religion you belong to. So— why only Jesus?

The position is considerably confused by the growing popularity of Eastern mysticism: Hare Krishna, transcendental meditation, Zen Buddhism, occultism and spiritism, and from time to time the startling claims of a religious leader such as the guru Maharaj Ji, "the Divine Light." Let us look at this particular prophet more closely, as his photograph is appearing on billboards and windows all over the world today.

The guru Maharaj Ji undoubtedly claims that he is the Christ for today. He accepts that Jesus, Mohammed, Krishna, Moses and others have been Divine Lights, or gurus, in the past; but they are all in the past and of the past, and everyone needs a perfect guru for today. According to the Maharaj Ji, his father had the True Knowledge of Divine Light, and now that same Knowledge and Light has been passed on to the son.

What are we to make of such claims? In the first place the Maharaj Ji quotes Jesus freely—and often inaccurately—and he is clearly trying to give the impression that he is expressing the modern counterpart of what Jesus said 2,000 years ago. If both are Divine Lights, this clearly must be so: "The Knowledge itself has always been the same." The trouble is that there are major and serious contradictions on most of the vital issues. For example, the Maharaj Ji says that God is not a person, but "cosmic energy"; Jesus said that God is so personal that we are to think of him as "our Father." The Maharaj Ji says that there is no sin, only "an active mind"; Jesus taught that sin was man's number one problem and indeed the basic cause of all the other problems in the world, a spiritual cancer that threatens to destroy us. The Maharaj Ji says that there is no atonement; Jesus declared that he came supremely "to give his life as a ransom for many," thereby taking away our sin and making reconciliation with God possible. The Maharaj Ji says that there is no resurrection; Jesus not only said that there is, not only claimed to be the resurrection and the life himself, but actually rose again from the dead to demonstrate the truth of his teaching. The Maharaj Ji says that there is no judgement; Jesus said that judgement is as certain as death, and much of his teaching was taken up with this solemn theme.

16

Whether or not you believe either teacher, it is quite impossible for *both* Jesus *and* the guru Maharaj Ji to possess the same divine knowledge and light, which is the guru's claim.

In the second place, and more simply, a high-caste Brahmin from India smiles at all the fuss made in the West concerning the Maharaj Ji. "In my country of India," he said, "there is nothing so special about him at all. We have many such people in India!" He is simply a much more intriguing figure for those of us who live in the West. Yet even in the West we should not be deceived so easily. Periodically a prophet arises, making startling claims and promises, deceiving a few thousand followers. The Korean Sun Myung Moon is another example. I am not wishing to dispute the personal sincerity of these men. But religious history is studded with numerous individuals who in turn have claimed to be "the Christ," "the guru," "the Divine Light" of their day; and Jesus himself warned us that "false Christs and false prophets will arise, and show great signs and wonders, so as to lead astray, if possible, even the elect."[8]

It is important to stress that Jesus did not say that all those of other faiths were wholly evil. Of course not! He recognized the love, beauty and truth that often did exist in those who were not his followers. Likewise, the Christian does not claim that he is always right and others always wrong, that he is always good and others always bad. Not at all! The light of God's truth has, in some measure, enlightened every man born into this world.

However, apart from certain general areas of agreement in the various religions and philosophies of the world, there are three absolutely crucial areas in which Jesus in unique.[9]

The uniqueness of his person

"Jesus went to the territory near the town of Caesarea Philippi, where he asked his disciples, 'Who do men say the Son of Man is?' 'Some say John the Baptist,' they answered. 'Others say Elijah, while others say Jeremiah or some other prophet.' "[10]

Today, virtually everyone would go as far as that: Jesus was one of the prophets, one of the great religious leaders of the world. I have never met anyone who has seriously disputed that. Though some would agree with Gandhi: Jesus is as divine as Krishna or Rama or Mohammed or Zoroaster—but no more.

That is the one thing you cannot say about Jesus!

Suppose, for example, you were present when I was speaking at a gathering of people. What would your reaction be if I said something like this in my address:

"Do you want to know what God is like? If you have seen me, you have seen God. I and God are one. I am the way to God. No one comes to God except by me. I am the Truth. I am the Life. I am the Light of the World. I am the Resurrection and the Life; if you believe in me you will never die eternally.

"I have the authority to forgive sins. One day I am coming back to this world, and I will judge all people of all time. Your future destiny depends entirely on your personal response to me and to my words. If you believe in me you already have eternal life; but if you do not obey me you will not see life and the wrath of God will rest upon you."

Further, suppose someone came up to me, kneeled

down before me, and, looking up in an attitude of worship, cried out, "My Lord and my God!" Suppose that I not only accepted his worship, but I gently rebuked him for being so slow to believe.

Moreover, if I went on making such statements, not only at that gathering, but constantly and repeatedly for the best part of three years—what then? You are left with two logical alternatives. *Either* this is outrageous blasphemy from someone who is mad or bad or worse. Of course if you do not believe in God it is hardly "blasphemy," but at least it would be outrageous nonsense. *Or*, these claims are true.

The one impossible conclusion is to say, "This man is a good religious teacher!" No *good* religious teacher has ever made or could make the claims that Jesus incessantly made for himself.

Others said, "That is the way. . . ."; Jesus said "I am the way." Others said, "That is the truth"; Jesus said "I am the truth." Others have pointed away from themselves to God; Jesus kept on saying, "Come to me . . . Follow me . . . I and my Father are one. . . ." Others said that they were messengers from God; Jesus said that he was himself the message. Indeed all that the prophets had spoken in the past was summed up in him. He was the Word made flesh, and that Word was God!

After the disciples had told Jesus that some were calling him "one of the prophets," Jesus went on to ask them, "What about you? Who do *you* say I am?" At once Simon Peter came back with the answer, "You are the Messiah, the Son of the living God." Jesus was obviously overjoyed by his spiritual perception, "Simon, son of John, you are happy indeed! For this truth did not come to you from any human being, but it was given to you directly by my Father in heaven."[11]

When Buddha was dying he was asked how people could best remember him. He urged his followers not to bother with that question. What mattered, he said, was his teaching and not his person. Christianity, however, is the only religion in the world which rests on the person of its Founder.

Of course anyone can make sweeping claims for himself; there is nothing very unique about that. But if I, for example, made such claims, my life would show the falsity of them within five minutes. And even if I could deceive a few strangers for a short time, ask those who know me best. Ask my wife! She could wax most eloquent on my faults and failings, and sometimes does! But now look at Jesus. Ask his closest friends, who saw him tired, harassed, misunderstood, pressured and persecuted. Peter said, "He was without blemish or spot." John said, "If we say we have no sin we deceive ourselves"; but of Jesus he said, "In him there is no sin."

Indeed, in Jesus you find a most perfect balance. He was sympathetic, but never weak; strong but never insensitive; loving but never indulgent; single-minded but never ruthless. Professor Anderson once put it like this: "He was a man not a woman, yet women as much as men find their perfect example in him. He was a Jew, not a European, African, or Indian; yet men and women of every race find in him all they would most wish to be."[12]

Further, if Jesus was and is the Son of God, he alone has the right to speak on all the greatest issues affecting each one of us: life and death, God and man, man's need in the sight of God, the way in which we can find God. You see, when it comes to these great questions, nobody knows the answer. Therefore whatever attitude anyone takes must be an attitude of faith. Ultimately this faith rests either in Christ, or in your personal opinion that what Christ says is not true. Thus when you become a true Christian, it is not a sudden leap of faith; you are simply transferring the object of your faith from your personal opinion (with all its uncertainty) to the person and authority and teaching of Jesus Christ. It is a great mistake to assume that the Christian has his head in the clouds, whilst the atheist or agnostic has his feet firmly on the ground. Concerning the great issues about life and death, we all have our head in the clouds, since no one *knows*. The Christian is simply calling to others to put their feet firmly on the rock of Jesus Christ. He alone is the one person worthy of our trust.

Moreover, everything about Christ endorses his claims that he has the right or the qualifications to speak on all these vital issues. If I have a pain in my chest, I may go to a friend who perhaps knows nothing about physical sickness. That friend might tell me that there is nothing really wrong, and I simply need to go to bed early, and all will be well tomorrow. However, I may go to a leading specialist, who warns me, after a series of very careful examinations, that I have a most serious disease and need an operation at once. Whatever advice I take, it is a matter of faith, but it is only sensible for me to put my trust in the one person who has the qualifications to speak. So it is with Jesus Christ.

Many people today feel no specific need of God; but

Jesus came in part to tell us about our need, and to explain most forcibly that we all have the fatal disease of sin which needs urgent and immediate treatment if we are to experience the life and health that only God can bring.

This brings us to the second unique feature of Jesus.

The uniqueness of his death

Although death is inevitable for each one of us, the death of Jesus has the greatest possible significance.

It is worth noticing that the first thing that John the Baptist said when he saw Jesus was, "Here is the Lamb of God who takes away the sin of the world."[13] For centuries God had taught his people that sin really matters to him. Sin is darkness, and God light: darkness and light do not mix. Sin always separates us from God. Further, for centuries God had taught his people that because sin really matters, and because God is holy and can have nothing sinful in his presence, there can be no forgiveness without sacrifice, usually the shedding of the blood of an animal. Most often it was the blood of a lamb. Now when John the Baptist declared that Jesus was the Lamb of God who had come to take away the sin of the world, he was referring to the coming sacrifice of Jesus on the cross, when he would bear the full weight of our sin, thus making it possible for us to be forgiven and accepted by God.

Again, the very first thing that Moses and Elijah discussed when they met with Jesus on the Mount of Transfiguration was "his departure (death), which he was to accomplish in Jerusalem." The word "accomplish" is an extraordinary word in the context. Whoever would talk about accomplishing his death? But when Jesus on the cross cried out "It is finished!" the word really means "accomplished." All that he had come to do, notably taking away the sin of the world, was now accomplished, or completed, or finished.

Again the very first thing that Jesus himself talked about when his disciples recognized him to be the Son of God was his coming death. "From that time on Jesus began to say plainly to his disciples: 'I must go to Jerusalem and suffer much from the elders, the chief priests, and the teachers of the Law. I will be put to death, and on the third day I will be raised to life.' Constantly he taught his disciples about his approaching death. Elsewhere he said that he had come into this world "to give his life as a ransom for many."[15] A ransom is the price paid to set a person free. How can we be free to know God? How can we be free from the guilt of sin? How can we be free to face death without fear, and especially the judgement after death? There is no answer at all, apart from the death of Jesus Christ.

Some philosophies today try to solve the problem by saying that there is no sin, and therefore no guilt, and that we are not responsible for our actions. However, those who shout most loudly about this are often those who shout most loudly about the rights and wrongs of society, and about the injustices in the world today. They show, by this, that they have indeed a very deep understanding of responsibility, guilt and justice. Well, if we demand justice, God also demands justice. He is far more concerned about this than we are. And there is no freedom from guilt, and no freedom from God's judgement apart from the death of Christ.

The uniqueness of his resurrection

Jesus predicted that "three days later he would be raised to life again." And he was! Not only was the tomb empty, which even his strongest opponents had to admit; not only was the risen Christ seen by at least 550 people on 11 separate occasions over a period of six weeks; not only was the evidence so conclusive that it convinced the doubting, disbelieving disciples, and transformed Saul of Tarsus, the arch-enemy of the Christian Church; but the same risen, living Lord Jesus has convinced and transformed millions of people right up to the present day. Some of them have been atheists and sceptics, until they were honest enough to face the facts.

We shall look at some of these facts later in the book, but at the beginning of Matthew 16 there is an interesting confrontation between the Pharisees and Jesus.

They came to test Jesus' claim of being the Messiah by asking him to show them some great demonstration in the skies. He replied, "When the sun is setting you say, 'We are going to have fine weather, because the sky is red.' And early in the morning you say, 'It is going to rain, because the sky is red and dark.' You can predict the weather by looking at the sky; but you cannot interpret the signs concerning these times! How evil and godless are the people of this day! You ask me for a miracle? No! The only miracle you will be given is the miracle of Jonah." Then he walked away.[16]

Here Jesus was calling their bluff. Some people are always protesting about lack of evidence, and demanding another sign. The truth is that there is abundant evidence for those who are willing to find Jesus. But very often those who do not believe do not *want* to believe. They do not want Jesus to interfere with their lives. All right, says Jesus, I won't interfere; but what will it profit you if you gain the whole world and lose your own life? Keep your world, if you want to; but you lose eternal life, and forgiveness, and God, and heaven, and everything of ultimate value!

One man, M. Lepeaux, once founded a religion which was meant to improve on Christianity. Finding no very great success, he talked to his wise friend Talleyrand. "There is one plan you might at least try," said his friend. "Why not be crucified and then rise again on the third day?"

Why only Jesus? Because no one else has claimed to be the Son of God and has justified his claims in every possible way. Because no one else has died for the sins of the world, making it possible for us to be absolutely forgiven. Because no one else has risen from the dead, no one else can give you any hope in the face of death, and no one else can offer you a living relationship with God himself. As Peter once said, "There is salvation in no one else, for there is no other name under heaven given among men by which we must be saved."[17]

The heart of the Christian faith is a personal relationship with Jesus Christ. Christianity is neither a philosophy, nor a code of ethics, nor social action. It may involve all three, but the essence of it all is to know Jesus personally, and through him to enter into a wonderful relationship with God himself.

Note on the authenticity and historicity of the New Testament documents
The cumulative evidence for the reliability of the New

Testament is powerful and weighty, and the person with serious doubts should study carefully *The New Testament Documents, Are they reliable?* by Professor F. F. Bruce.[18] However, we should bear in mind the following points: (a) We have about 5,000 Greek manuscripts in existence, some of which date back to the second century, or even the late first century, A.D. And among the differences in the manuscripts there is not a single dispute about any basic doctrine. Compare this with other ancient histories. The oldest manuscript of the historian Tacitus comes 800 years after the original; and that of Thucydides, 1,300 years. Yet most scholars would accept these single manuscripts as reliable historical documents!

(b) Where historical details in the New Testament can be verified by other writings or archaeological discoveries, again and again they are found to be accurate. Dr. Luke, for example, the author of the Gospel and the Acts of the Apostles, gives astonishing and painstaking details about all sorts of political, historical, geographical and nautical records, and their verification establish him as a thoroughly accurate chronicler. There is no reason, therefore, to doubt other details which cannot be verified so easily.

(c) Although the first of the Gospels was written some thirty years after the death of Jesus, we must remember the following:

(i) The power of oral tradition was very strong—as it still is today in parts of the world where there is little or no access to written material.

(ii) Jesus taught in Aramaic, in a poetic style which is highly memorable, probably requiring his disciples to learn his teachings by heart, as did most other

Rabbis.

(iii) *Somebody* said those magnificent words, because we have them in black and white before us in our Bibles. And whoever said them was a genius.

(iv) There were many eye-witnesses alive when the first of the Gospels were written. Most disciples were passionately jealous of the truth about Jesus. There is no evidence that any disciples ever questioned the authenticity or accuracy of the Gospel records. No one tried to discredit them.

At the very least we should accept them as reliable historical documents, an authentic account of the life and teaching of Jesus of Nazareth.

[1]*The God I want.* (Constable), page 21f.

[2]Op. cit., page 107

[3]John 14:6 (TEV)

[4]John 14:9 (TEV)

[5]Hebrews 1:1f (TEV)

[6]John 1. 1:14 (TEV)

[7]Quoted in *Christianity & Comparative Religion,* by J. N. D. Anderson (Inter-Varsity).

[8]Matthew 24:24

[9]For a note on the authenticity and historicity of the New Testament documents see the end of this chapter.

[10]Matthew 16:13-14 (TEV)

[11]Matthew 16: 15-17 (TEV)

[12]*Christianity the Witness of History* (IVP), page 51

[13]John 1:29 (TEV)

[14]Matthew 16:21 (TEV)

[15]Mark 10:45

[16]Matthew 16:2-4

[17]Acts 4:12

[18]Eerdmans. Also, for more popular reading, *Runaway World* by Michael Green (Inter-Varsity); *The Ring of Truth* by J. B. Phillips (Macmillan); *Christianity the Witness of History* by J. N. D. Anderson (IVP).

2

FRUSTRATION, APATHY, VIOLENCE

Few things are more obvious in today's restless society than frustration. We see it in the mental illnesses which torment a growing number of the population, in the industrial tensions which are rife everywhere, in the deadlock in Northern Ireland, indeed almost everywhere you look. There is hardly a section in society, or a country in the world, free from frustration. In the musical *Hair* there is a song, which has as its constant refrain, "Is there an answer? Tell me why, tell me why, tell me why . . . ." The areas of frustration are well known.

First, there is *frustration about the future*. Fifty years ago, men boasted of the irresistible progress of mankind.

Glory to Man in the highest,
For Man is the master of things.

Utopia was around the corner. Today no one says anything so foolish. Most of the leading experts are extremely pessimistic. The computer scientist Professor J. Forrestor of the Massachusetts Institute of Technology a short time ago fed into the computers the relevant data of our time: population, pollution, capital investments, technology, natural resources, quality of life, and food production. Out came the prediction that civilization has perhaps one generation to survive. In many informed circles there is an atmosphere of total frustration. Man has no answers. The Prophets of Doom today are not theologians but scientists.

The atomic bomb in Hiroshima in 1945 killed 87,000 people in one second. The hydrogen bomb, tested seven years later, was a thousand times stronger. Only two years after that, tests with the cobalt bomb proved that the destruction of all life on earth is possible. The explosion of a cobalt bomb would produce a radio-active cloud whose degree of destruction would be three hundred thousand times stronger than the first hydrogen bomb, which in turn, was a thousand times stronger than the first atomic bomb. Mankind has now sufficient nuclear explosives in the world to eliminate itself fifty thousand times over. Indeed, there is the equivalent of 10 tons of TNT for every man, woman and child on this earth. Further, scientists are in the process of producing a biological bomb of devastating power. And in the history of mankind there never has yet been a weapon invented by man which has not been used, sooner or later.

The facts about pollution are equally alarming. The average American has 12 parts per million DDT in his fatty tissues. If that means nothing to you, let me add that meat with only seven parts DDT is considered unfit to eat! Many scientists today think that all life on earth is imperilled by DDT pollution alone. Water pollution due to industrial waste is equally appalling. Most notorious is Lake Erie. In 1956 the blue pike catch alone came to just short of 7,000,000 lbs. Today if you were to fall into the lake by accident, you would be advised to have a tetanus injection.

The population explosion is yet another matter of extreme urgency. Within 30 years the population of the world will double. Yet already, more than 30,000,000 people die of hunger each year. Arthur Koestler has said "Human civilization is either on the verge of, or in the process of, exploding."

A 6th grade girl expressed her dismay at world events like this:

If I were the sun
And I saw the things that people had done
I would eclipse myself
Forever.[1]

Second, there is *frustration about technology*. Clearly the build-up of nuclear weapons, the pollution of our environment, and the population bomb, are all directly caused by the astonishing "progress" in science and technology. We build mindless machines, which then threaten our very existence. Charles Reich in *The Greening of America* talks about these mindless machines, or the progress of technology, in these words: "They pulverize everything in their power: the landscape, the natural environment, history and tradition, the amenities and civilities, the privacy and spaciousness of life, beauty, the fragile, the slow growing social structures which bind us together. Organization and bureaucracy, which are applications of technology to social institutions, increasingly dictate how we shall live our lives, with the logic of organization taking precedence over any other value."[2]

Moreover, the Professor of Psychology and Psychiatry in the University of Chicago, Dr. Bruno Bettelheim, a man who once suffered in the concentration camps of Dachau and Buchenwald, says that the frustration of today, which is so often outwardly expressed in terms of political or social issues is really the frustration that "youth has no future." "Modern technology has made them obsolete. They have become socially irrelevant and, as persons, insignificant. Not because their future is bleak with a prospect of a nuclear holocaust, but because of their feeling that nobody needs them, that society can do nicely without them. . . . Their anxiety is not (as they claim) about an impending atomic war. It is not that society has no future. Their existential anxiety is that they have no future in a society that does not need them to go on existing. It is modern technology—with its automation and computerization—that seems to make man and his work obsolete, seems to rob him of his personal importance in the scheme of things."[3]

Thus the battle against the war machine is really the battle against the machine, because the machine, and all that goes with it in terms of bureaucracy and organization, tends to dominate human life. We are faced today with the same sort of frustration on a massive scale that some mill-workers felt in the 19th century when the machine threatened to destroy personal significance and the value of the individual. What is the meaning of man when trips to the moon have become almost commonplace and a third of the world is left starving?

Third, there is a *frustration about jobs and studies*. Many students, for example, have told me of the frustration that they feel about having to concentrate on some narrow, specialized area of academic study which seems totally unrelated to the huge and urgent problems of today. Why bother? Why be pressured into exams or degrees? Of what ultimate value is social status or financial reward? And even those are no longer guaranteed. Satisfying jobs seem increasingly hard to find. Strikes and redundancies are part of the daily scene.

A girl told me that she asked her humanist boyfriend, "Why are you acting all the time? You never seem to be your real self." He replied that if he stopped acting, life would become so meaningless that he could no longer live.

In the fourth place there is much *frustration with religion*. An increasing number today are searching for a spiritual solution to some of these problems, but, once again, many become perplexed and disillusioned. After all, the Church as a whole is not noted for its spiritual vitality. Although the organized structure of the Church has often been compared with scaffold surrounding a building, this scaffolding has apparently become so rusty that it cannot be moved and the existence of the living temple of the Church seems open to doubt. So much of the organized religion of our day "seems as if God is dead and our lives have become an indefinite waiting for an explanation that never comes."

"Oh God, if you exist at all, where are you? Why don't you answer me? Why are you so silent? My soul thirsts for God, for the living God. . . ." And some, finding no reply, turn their backs on the Christian faith and become agnostics, atheists or humanists.

The curious thing is that even an atheist cannot get rid of spiritual hunger. A person may deny that food exists: but that will not stop him from being physically hungry. Similarly, a person may deny that God exists: but that will not prevent him from being hungry spiritually. Hence the frustration when religion does not seem to satisfy this basic spiritual hunger.

Now in the light of this world of frustration, there are two extremely common reactions. Most widespread of all is *apathy*. "During World War II, a bearded Chindit soldier, fighting with General Wingate's forces behind the Japanese lines in Burma, actually fell asleep while a storm of machine-gun bullets splattered around him. Subsequent investigation revealed that this soldier was not merely reacting to physical fatigue from lack of sleep, but surrendering to a sense of overpowering apathy."[5] In other words, with his immediate situation so chaotic and alarming, his only protection from fear, panic or depression was total apathy. Who cares?

In the same book as the foregoing incident, Alvin Toffler talks about the bewildering change which is accelerating all the time. Many people, he says, cannot cope rationally with change, so they fall into "drug-induced lassitude, video-induced stupor, alcoholic haze—when the old vegetate and die in loneliness."[6]

The main trouble with apathy, of course, is that nothing is solved, neither the problems nor the frustrations. We may repress our frustrations, and cover them up with an air of euphoria, and say that "all is well." However, the problems remain, and just beneath the surface the frustrations are very much there, often becoming one of the major causes of depression which is so prevalent today. Every year over 30 million days are lost in industry in Britain alone due to depression and nervous disorders, far more than the total time lost in strikes. The National Health Service Bill for tranquilizers and pep pills runs at about 130,000,000 pounds a year. Such figures are a small measure of the frustrations experienced in society today.

The second reaction to frustration is protest, which increasingly today is leading to *violence*. With problems so vast that solutions seem out of the question, many are saying that "the only thing left is to bring down the whole system. With society so rotten, it can neither reform itself nor be reformed, but can only be born again through violent revolution."[7] Jerry Rubin, the Yippie organiser, protested, "Who the hell wants to make it in America anymore? The American economy no longer needs young whites and blacks. We are waste material. We fulfil our destiny in life by rejecting a system which rejects us."[8]

The only trouble with violent protests and revolutions is not that they change too much, but that they change too little. They fail entirely to affect the very nature of man, which is the ultimate cause of frustration. For example, the Czarist regime in Russia, corrupt and oppressive as it undoubtedly was and an immense cause of frustration amongst the workers, gave way to the Communist regime and to men like Stalin, who has been called the greatest mass murderer in human history. An Eastern European once made the shrewd comment that the only difference between capitalism and communism is that with capitalism man exploits man; and with communism the reverse is the case! Violence is nearly always an unbearably frustrating answer to frustration.

Indeed the reason why both apathy and violence fail entirely to satisfy is this. The basic frustration is with myself. This is where the real problem lies: in myself, in my heart, in my innermost being. My whole attitude towards society, towards both God and man, may be wrong. A student psychiatrist, who for many years had tried to help extremists and militants who were in difficulties, said this: "Psychologically I find most student extremists hating themselves as intensely as they hate the establishment—a self-hatred they try to escape from by fighting any establishment."[9] Moreover, when the outward objective is reached, with university regulations changed or peace in Vietnam, this often adds to the frustration. Because when the object of frustration is removed, the raw truth about frustration is seen as it really is: I am frustrated, not because of him, her, them or it, primarily, but because of *me*. I am the basic problem! And that is the problem which is so overwhelming! An old saying puts it like this: "The man who goes out to change society is an optimist. The man who goes out to change society without changing the individual is a lunatic!"

That is why Jesus Christ is so utterly relevant for today. He comes to deal with the individual. He comes to change our heart and our nature. He is concerned with our attitudes first and foremost, not principally with our situation. And of course when our attitudes are changed, often our situation is considerably changed as well. But even if the pressures and problems are exactly the same, Jesus is the One who can transform the whole scene by his living presence with us. In fact, Jesus alone has the answer to the most basic cries of modern man. What are these cries?

The cry for meaning

First, there is the *cry for meaning and purpose*. Of course, there is nothing new about this: 3,000 years ago a preacher said, "Emptiness, emptiness, emptiness, all is empty. What does man gain from all his labor and his toil here under the sun? To what purpose have I been wise? What is the profit of it? Even this is emptiness. So I came to hate life, since everything that was done here under the sun was a trouble to me; for all was emptiness and chasing the wind."[10]

However, this is thought to be the most poignant cry of today, and the root cause of most of our restlessness and frustration. According to Jean-Paul Sartre, "Here we are, all of us, eating and drinking to preserve our precious existence, and . . . there is nothing, nothing, absolutely no reason for existing."

I talked with an ex-heroin addict in Vancouver, who had been bound by heroin for three years but who had been wonderfully set free by Jesus Christ. He told me what I have so often been told, "I took drugs because life was so completely futile and empty. I was searching for personal significance." A university professor told me that an increasing number of mature men were coming to him depressed or in despair: "Outwardly, it might be a case of job frustration; but inwardly they are all desperately searching for some ultimate meaning to life."

Psychiatrists like Dr. Victor Frankl of the University of Vienna call this the "existential vacuum." More and more people are coming into consulting rooms and clinics complaining of an inner emptiness, a sense of total and ultimate meaninglessness of life. Dr. Frankl has devised a "logotherapy," or existential analysis, to help patients to put meaning into their otherwise meaningless existence.

Jesus, knowing this basic need of man, kept on saying to people "Follow me! follow me! I am the light of the world. He who follows me shall not walk in darkness, but shall have the light of life." A mother wrote to me a little time ago like this: "I will never forget January 13th when you helped me to accept Christ as my Savior and Lord. During those two weeks you made me understand where I was going. I was simply going through life like a blind person who didn't even want to see. Now it is wonderful to have a Friend so near me all the time." Today she has found the glorious purpose and life that only Jesus can bring.

The cry for love
Second, there is the *cry for love*. Loneliness, as well as emptiness, is an acute problem of today. Part of the temporary popularity of the Beatles came from the huge relevance of such songs as Eleanor Rigby:

Ah, look at all the lonely people,
Look at all the lonely people.
Where do they all come from?
Where do they all belong?

So many people today want to be wanted, they long to belong. In a survey amongst students, 86 percent said that their main problem was loneliness. Most of us, if not all of us, will know this from time to time.

The reason is basic. The real and important world is the world inside us, not the world outside. In my outside world, I may know hundreds and thousands of people. There they are, all around me every day. Yet in my inside world, if there is no love, I shall be lonely.

One young person, in desperate need, wrote to me about "a great absence in my life—an empty silence within."

However, Jesus offers a quality of love that will satisfy our inside world. The Spirit of Jesus can come to live within us, in our innermost being. God's love, wrote Paul, is poured into our hearts by the Holy Spirit. Jesus once talked to a woman who was trying to find satisfaction from sexual relationships. She had lived with six men, and still was lonely. Jesus answered: "Whoever drinks this water will get thirsty again; but whoever drinks the water that I will give him will never be thirsty again. For the water that I will give him will become in him a spring which will provide him with living water, and give him eternal life."[11]

A university student who, until recently, was a cynical atheist wrote to me, "I had tried praying with no apparent effect—which to a very cynical atheist indeed is a pretty strong confirmation of why not to believe in a living God. And then came [a special service]. I cannot describe what I felt or what I feel now, but I know that I have been privileged to realize and recognize what being forgiven and accepted by Jesus means. The wonder of it all amazes me, overwhelms me, and words fail to express the joy of realizing that I am never alone, never forgotten."

Martin Niemöller, incarcerated in concentration camps for many years, had only one possession, a Bible. He wrote: "The Bible: what did this book mean to me during the long and weary years of solitary confinement, and then for the last four years at Dachau Cell-Building? The Word of God was simply everything to me—comfort and strength, guidance and hope, master of my days and companion of my nights, the Bread which kept me from starvation, and the Water of life which refreshed my soul. And even more: 'solitary confinement' ceased to be solitary."

Jesus alone can fully answer that cry for love. He loves us more than anyone could ever love us. He will never fail us, nor forsake us. Moreover, we belong not only to him, but to his family all over the world. He wants us to enter in to depths of relationships and love which come from God himself.

The cry for freedom

Third, there is a *cry for freedom*. All too often today people blame their situation for their problems in life. "If only we had a different government . . . if only I had a different husband/wife . . . if only something were different, all would be different." But nearly always, it is not primarily our situation; it is our *reaction to the situation* that counts. The thing that really hurts is my pride, my jealousy, my resentment, my self-pity. These are the most frustrating things in life.

Jesus promised, "If the Son makes you free, then you will be really free."[12] God promised in the Old Testament, "A new heart I will give you and a new spirit I will put within you; and I will take out of your flesh the heart of stone and give you a heart of flesh."[13] God wants to take away our stony, selfish, frustrated heart, and to give us instead a heart of love.

Recently I visited a prisoner called John, in one of Britain's top security prisons. John had a reputation of being one of the worst of the prisoners, consumed with bitterness and hatred for the police in particular and for society in general. He frequently made protests of one form or another. Sometimes he slashed his wrists. On one of these occasions, he thought he was dying, and in that moment of panic cried out to Jesus for help and forgiveness. At once Jesus came to set him free! God gave him a new heart and put a new spirit within him. I found John to be a most loving and gentle and peaceful prisoner when I saw him. It was a miracle! Later on he wrote to me this letter:

"This is my fifth time in prison and I am serving eight years for fraud. . . . I was dirty outside my body as I never used to wash. I was dirty inside my heart, lust, hatred, greed, revenge, anger and malice. . . . [Then he explained how he called out to Jesus for help.] All my pains, worries and burdens left me. I was able to stop smoking. I was able to stop reading dirty books. I was able to stop using dirty words; and greatest of all I was able to love the people whom I had hated. I felt a completely different person, like being born again, and this is the great work of our Lord Jesus Christ. I was really cleaned inside out. . . . For the first time in my life, I am a free man—free of sin, free of the filth that has been inside me for years. The truth has made me free, the truth being the Lord Jesus Christ."

Here is a man serving eight years in prison, and yet able to say sincerely that he is a "free man." Only Jesus can answer the deep cry for freedom that is in the heart of man.

Take the case of Tom Skinner, one-time leader of a tough Negro gang in New York, who was set free by the power of Christ. Shortly after his conversion, he was attacked quite unfairly by a white man. Tom Skinner records, "I hit the ground, as he kicked me, shouting, 'You dirty black nigger! I'll teach you a thing or

41

two!' I got up and heard myself saying, 'You know, because of Jesus Christ I love you.' " Here was a potentially violent man, and formerly a totally frustrated man, who had received the power to love his enemies. When we find Christ our situation may not immediately change, but our reactions, attitudes and habits can radically change. Only Jesus can do that.

The cry for forgiveness

Fourth, there is the *cry for forgiveness*. A student once described man's predicament to me like this: "There is no one in the universe with the authority to forgive." Indeed, this fact of guilt and this need of forgiveness involves us all. We are all guilty in God's eyes; we have broken his laws and rebelled against him. And Jesus taught repeatedly that man's greatest problem was sin and his greatest need was forgiveness. Like the prodigal son[14] we have all gone our own way, to lead our lives as we wish, and then find ourselves cut off from the only one who really loves and cares for us. Sin always separates us from God. There is a verse in the Bible which warns us that some of the consequences of sin will be "confusion and frustration."[15]

I once talked to a university student, a girl who had a reputation as "the toughest girl in our university." She had slept around freely, and taken every known drug on the campus. Outwardly she didn't care about anything and seemed quite hardened against the Christian faith. After a meeting she came up to me, still smoking, to say that she had asked Christ into her life as her Savior and Lord. My immediate reaction was "time will tell." However, the next night she came to me again, and I hardly recognized her as being the same person. She told me about her first 24 hours as a Christian. She had spent most of that day crying. For years and years, she explained, in spite of her toughness and hardness, she felt "as guilty as hell." No one would have guessed it, but on that Sunday all her guilt had been coming out and she was overwhelmed by the love of Jesus. She could not really believe that he loved her, and had died for her, and had taken away all her sins. It was wonderful for her to experience complete forgiveness. Another person wrote to me, "I already feel a wonderful sense of freedom, as if a great weight has been taken off my shoulders." God not only forgives, he forgets. "Your sins and iniquities I will remember no more."

The cry for hope

Fifth, there is a *cry for hope*. What hope has anyone in the face of death, apart from Jesus Christ? What hope can anyone give? What assurance can we possibly have, apart from Christ? But through the death and resurrection of Christ, with all the solid, historical evidence for that, there is a glorious answer to this cry for hope.

Jo was a lovely Christian girl, aged twenty, but dying from leukemia. Three days before her death her father wrote me this letter, "All treatment for Jo has been stopped. Medically she has been given a few days only. She knows the situation, is quite calm and is praying to Jesus. . . ."

I heard from Jo's father again just after her funeral. "Although so very weak and becoming more and more delirious, I know she died full of faith; and literally, but for the last few moments, held her right hand pointing up to Jesus as she could not speak. . . . In spite of all our sorrow it was wonderful seeing her coming closer and closer to Jesus. . . . We never forget that Jo is now with him and we would not want to disturb her happiness, even if we could. . . . Jo had a wonderful 'funeral.' The church was packed, and we all praised the Lord with hands raised. . . . 'Bless the Lord O my soul, and let all that is within me bless his holy name.' " Who else can give you such hope in the face of death? There is no one apart from Jesus Christ.

The cry for God

Finally, there is a *cry for God*. In spite of the frustration with religion and the deadness of much of the Church, many are still hungry for God and for spiritual reality. Jesus made it plain, "Whoever has seen me has seen the Father . . . I am the way, I am the truth, I am the life; no one goes to the Father except by me."[16] Therefore God becomes real only when we find Jesus and enter into a personal relationship with him. That is the heart of it all. It is not only God's answer to frustration; it is God's supreme purpose for our life; that we should know him and experience his love through a personal relationship with his son Jesus Christ. This is where we must start in our search for God.

[1] Quoted in *Pornography, The Longford Report* (Coronet), page 347

[2] Op. cit. (Bantam Books © Charles A. Reich, 1970. Reprinted by permission of Bantam Books.

[3] *Encounter,* September 1969, page 31

[4] *Waiting for Godot,* Samuel Becket (Grove)

[5] *Future Shock,* Alvin Toffler (Bantam Books)

[6] Op. cit.

[7] *Encounter,* September 1969, page 30

[8] Op. cit., page 33

[9] *Encounter,* September 1969, page 36

[10] Ecclesiastes 1:2f, 2:15, 17 (NEB)

[11] John 4:13f (TEV)

[12] John 8:36 (TEV)

[13] Ezekiel 36:26

[14] See Luke 15: 11ff

[15] Deuteronomy 28:20

[16] John 14:9, 6 (TEV)

3
WHY IS MAN?

At the University of Illinois, the College of Fine and Applied Arts has tried to humanize today's trend towards computerization. Each quarter the administration sends out a card to check the students' schedule. The accompanying letter begins something like this: "Dear 344-28-0430: We have a personal interest in you."

Here we have the major personal crisis of today: not "What is man?" but "Why is man?" Has man any ultimate meaning or purpose at all? You see, the human predicament is simply this. If there is no God then there is no ultimate meaning to life. If God is dead, man is dead. "Man is a completely futile being"—without God. This is what so many writers and philosophers and artists are saying today. I once asked a well-known opera singer about some of the more avant-garde music of today. "Well," she said, "I am not too impressed with some of that. It is the music of man disturbed, confused, restless—man who has lost meaning and purpose because God is not real."

If the primary question were "What is man?" then, of course, there are many answers which could be summarized roughly in these well-known definitions. As to his size, man is "nothing but an accidental coincidence on a minor speck of interstellar dust." As to his component parts, man is "nothing but fat enough for seven bars of soap, iron enough for one medium-sized nail, sugar enough to sweeten seven cups of coffee, lime enough to whitewash one chicken coop, phosphorus enough to tip 2,200 matches, magnesium enough for one dose of salts, potash enough to explode one toy crane, and sulphur enough to rid one dog of fleas."

As to his mechanism, he is "nothing but complex bio-chemical mechanism powered by a combustion system which energizes computers with prodigious storage facilities for retaining encoded information." As to his appearance man is "nothing but a naked ape."

The trouble with these "nothing but" definitions is that according to your own view, once you have fully and accurately described man in terms of, say, "a complex bio-chemical mechanism . . .", the impression is given that there is nothing more to be said. However, suppose you go into a beautiful village and take with you an architect, a painter, a poet, a historian, and an engineer, and ask each one to fully and comprehensively describe the village, you would have five very different impressions. All would be equally valid, each would complement the other. No one could say that the village was "nothing but" their particular description. Tell a TV audience that Miss World is "nothing but a complex bio-chemical mechanism," and I think most of them will disagree. Or, if you like, put a shining, streamlined, modern computer in place of Miss World, and see if you get the same viewing audience!

However, many share the view of humanist Dr. Edmund Leach who rejects any thought of man as a special creation by God, and says that "there is no sharp break of continuity between what is human and what is mechanical."[1]

Now, if that were true, if there were no ultimate meaning to life, why bother about anything at all? For example, why get worked up about justice? Why protest about social or racial inequity? How could I be fair or unfair, just or unjust, to what is basically a machine? If man were only a machine, determined biologically or psychologically, then why be concerned about any political, social, racial or legal issue at all? If man is less than a created being, anything goes.

She was beautifully, delicately made,
So still, so unafraid,
Till the bomb came,
Bombs are the same,
Beautifully, delicately made.[2]

What is the difference between "she" and "it"? If man were simply a cog in a vast soul-less machine, the individual would be completely expendable: he or she would be a means to an end, an object to be used. It is, of course, a common philosophy of today, shared by Marxists, nihilists,[3] and pornographers. If Marx's dictum were true, that "the material world to which we belong is the only reality," then anything goes. Dr. Viktor Frankl, who survived the Auschwitz concentration camp, says that the nihilistic philosophies of the 19th century led to the death camps of the 20th century, and that even now there is a "nihilist tendency to devalue and depreciate that which is human in man." Whether for sex or violence, men and women often tragically use one another. In an "exclusive" interview with a well-known British newspaper, Raquel Welch is reported to have said, "I am just a piece of meat . . . I fulfil the ambitions of other people to make money out of me." The article was titled "The Torment of the World's Number One Sex Symbol."

Carry this philosophy to its logical extremes and you can do what you like with a slab of meat or with a human machine. And for that matter, other human machines can do what they like with you! Nothing is fair or unfair. There is no justice, there are no rights or wrongs, there are no safeguards of any kind, if man is simply a machine. Some existentialist thinkers[4] are saying that it is as meaningless to run down an old woman in your car as it is to give her a ride. It is important to see the logical implications of such a philosophy. All human values, personal considerations, love, caring, sharing, compassion, justice, honesty and friendship vanish if man is fundamentally a machine.

Practically speaking, of course, it is quite impossible to live consistently with this philosophy. We attach meaning to almost everything we do. We have friends, we make love, we care about justice and injustice. We would not tolerate old women being run over with brave existentialist abandon! We protest many things. We make value-judgements about one another. We are not indifferent to Hitler's massacre of six million Jews or Stalin's murder of 20 million people. If we really believed in complete determinism, all these values would be meaningless. Indeed most of our time we live, love, think and act so unlike mere machines that you find Jean-Paul Sartre, for example, saying, "Man is absurd, but he must grimly act as if he were not!"

Why is man? The answer in the first place is to see him in relation to a Creator God. It is important to understand that if there is an infinite personal God at all, he must be infinitely greater than man's total understand. Therefore we can know God only if he reveals himself to us, and breaks into our circle of understanding. And the Christian contention is that there is such a God, that he has revealed himself to us in a great variety of ways, one of which is creation itself.

Professor Tony Holland, Professor of Chemical Engineering in the University of Salford, was a scientific humanist up to the age of about thirty. Then, in his own words, "The first question I asked was 'Is there a God?' On consideration, it was inconceivable to me that the complex system of which we are a part could have occurred without a Creator. Just as a great symphony testifies to the skill of the composer, the world and the universe testify to the wisdom and power of God. Science is but a description of God's work."

Professor Edwin Carlstin, biologist at Princeton University, has said "The probability of life originating from accident is comparable to the probability of the Unabridged Dictionary resulting from an explosion in a printing factory." Certainly the complexity, beauty, exquisite design, and purposefulness of creation points directly towards a Creator and Designer. Not that creation is a watertight *proof* of God's existence, but at least it is a pointer. Of course there is much clearer evidence in the person of Jesus Christ, God's supreme revelation of himself: "The Word became a human being." Now in the light of the existence of a Creator God, several facts about man become clear.

The smallness of man

At times it is important to remember just how small we are. Franklin D. Roosevelt used to have a little ritual with the famous naturalist, William Beebe. After an evening's chat the two men would go outside and look into the night sky. Gazing into the stars, they would find the lower lefthand corner of the great square of Pegasus. One of them would recite these words, as part of their ritual: "That is a spiral galaxy of Andromeda. It is as large as our Milky Way. It is one of a hundred million galaxies. It is 750,000 light-years away. It consists of 100 billion suns, each larger than our sun." They would then pause, and Roosevelt would finally say, "Now I think we feel small enough. Let us go to bed!"

King David, seeing the night sky studded with stars, once exclaimed, "Oh Lord, our Lord, how majestic is thy name in all the earth . . .! When I look at thy heavens, the work of thy fingers, the moon and the stars which thou hast established; what is man that thou art mindful of him, and the son of man that thou dost care for him?"[5] The Bible speaks about man as having been created from the dust: "You are dust, and to dust you shall return."

It is necessary for us at times to be cut down to size. There is in some circles today an arrogance in thinking about God, as though the basic question were, "Why should I bother with God?" The real question is, of course, "Why should God bother with me?" That is a much harder question to answer. In the words of the prophet Isaiah, "Behold, the nations are like a drop from a bucket, and are accounted as the dust on the scales; behold he takes up the isles like fine dust. . . . All the nations are as nothing before him, they are counted by him as less than nothing and emptiness. To whom then will you liken God, or what likeness compare with him? . . . Have you not known? Have you not heard? The Lord is the everlasting God, the Creator of the ends of the earth."[6]

Some people assume that we have a right to God's love. They see man at the centre of the universe; and God, if he exists at all, is simply there to give us our rights and to meet all our needs. And if God is able to satisfy my ideas about him, and my ideas about life, justice or love, then I might perhaps consider believing in him, as though I were doing him a favor. What some fail to realize completely is that *God is at the centre* of the universe. The question is not "Is God relevant to me?" but "Am I relevant to God?" How can *we*, tiny, sinful, rebellious human beings, have any contact with an infinite, personal God who is utterly holy? When it comes to man's rights before God, the only thing that we can say is that we have the right to be judged. Many times it says in the Bible "God resists the proud;" and if we come with all our intellectual guns firing away with arrogant arguments, we shall never, never find God.

However, since there is a Creator God who has made man in his own image, we come face to face with another most important fact.

The significance of man
Each individual, rebellious and sinful though he may

be, is of tremendous significance in the sight of the Creator God. Being made in the image of God, man has at least five characteristics which are not shared by the rest of the animal creation. Man can reason, and reflect; he can choose, as a free agent; he can love, consciously preferring one above another; and above all he can worship God and know God, and thus becomes personally responsible to his Creator. He is meant to live in complete dependence upon God. Indeed the whole point of the Genesis 1 account of creation is that man is seen, not as the ape, but as the apex of creation. Some people are worried about the six days of creation. But quite apart from the fact that "day" in Hebrew thought is simply a period of time, the main point, I believe, is that man is so much the crown of creation that the rest of the creation of the universe is as only five days in comparison!

That is why is it wrong to use one another, to kill, to neglect, or exploit one another. Each individual human being has been made in God's own image. There is no philosophy in the world that gives such dignity and significance to man as the Christian faith. Indeed it is precisely because of this that Christians have always been in the forefront of social justice. It is Christians who have freed the slaves, emancipated women, cared for the sick, instituted Trade Unions, and brought education, medicine and principals of justice to oppressed people all over the world. Of course Christians have also made countless mistakes, and "religion," as opposed to the real thing, can be appalingly cruel and heartless. But wherever individual Christians and groups of Christians experience the love of God, this love will inevitably spill out in compassion towards the numerous needs of man.

However, it is because of the enormous significance of the individual in the sight of God, that we must also consider a third factor.

The sinfulness of man

Jesus taught repeatedly that the evils of this world can all ultimately be traced back to the fall of man, to the sinful nature of our hearts. In Ephesians 2:1 Paul reminds the Christians at Ephesus about their true spiritual condition, before God made them alive in Christ: "You were dead through your trespasses and sins." It is not that *God* is dead, as some are thinking and saying today; but that spiritually *we* are dead to God, which is a very different matter. Because of "trespasses and sins" we do not naturally enjoy the living relationship with God; he is not real in our experience.

There are two main characteristics of a dead person, either physically or spiritually. First he is *helpless*. After all, what can a dead body do? Nothing except rot! Likewise a spiritually dead person is helpless to do the things he ought to do because, says Paul, he follows or is controlled by three things.

In the first place, he follows the course of this world: "You drifted along on the stream of this world's ideas of living" (J. B. Phillips translation). Most people drift with the crowd, as a dead piece of wood floats down the river. How easily we are governed by the world around us! Keeping up with our neighbors, or with our particular social set or group is a very powerful principle. Various people tell me how they cheat on their income tax returns, or fool around in ways that are illegal or immoral, but quickly add the rejoinder, "Well, everybody's doing it!" The subtlety is this: we think that we can play with the world as we like. No, says Paul, the stream of this world is carrying you along. Elsewhere he says "The world is trying to squeeze you into its own mold."[8] And it is frankly a mouldy mold, because it will take you right away from the living God. However, the spiritually dead person is helpless to prevent this.

In the second place, says Paul, the spiritually dead person follows the prince of the power of the air. We shall look at this thought more closely in a later chapter, but the New Testament teaches clearly that the whole world lies under the control of Satan whenever or wherever Christ is not personally accepted as King: "The whole world is under the rule of the Evil One"[9] Satan is called "the god of this world."[10] We see this, of course, in all the forms of occult practice which are very much on the increase, but we also see Satan's activity in every part of life which seeks to draw people away from God's Son Jesus Christ: materialism, greed, and even entertainment or sport. The 1968 Gallup poll over Western Europe, from 10,000 interviews, came to six conclusions:

1. Religious beliefs are declining.
2. Morals have also slumped.
3. Honesty is on the wane.
4. Happiness is becoming increasingly hard to find.
5. Peace of mind is rare.
6. Hardly anybody believes in the Devil: "the Devil has had it."

However, it is quite clear that Jesus believed in a personal Devil, and warned groups of people that they were under his control: "You are the children of your father, the Devil"[11] Naturally the spiritually dead person is controlled by the prince of the power of the air, and is helpless to do anything about it.

In the third place, the spiritually dead person follows the desires of body and mind, or the passions of the flesh. In the New Testament "flesh" refers to our self-life: selfishness, self-centredness, self-seeking, and all manifestations of self. William Temple once explained that this is the fundamental meaning of sin; "I am the centre of the world I see: where the horizon is depends on where I stand.... Education may make my self-centredness less disastrous by widening my horizon of interests: so far it is like climbing a tower, which widens the horizon for physical vision, while leaving me still the centre and standard of reference." Once again, the spiritually dead person is helpless to do anything about this.

Then, the second mark of a dead person is that he is *separated* from other people. In physical death this separation is obvious and is the cause of sadness and bereavement. But spiritual death is even more serious. It not only brings separation between man and man, (hence all the tensions and problems in society), it brings a separation between man and God. Paul wrote to the Ephesian Christians, "Remember that you were at that time [before your conversion] separated from Christ, alienated from the commonwealth of Israel, and strangers to the covenants of promise, having no hope and without God in the world."[12] Here he uses five words or phrases to express this estrangement: separated, alienated, strangers, no hope, without God. This separation from God now will one day become a full, final and eternal separation from God and from all good. This is what Christ called "outer darkness," "a great gulf fixed," "hell." Perhaps the most disturbing feature about this is its absolute fairness. The essence of judgement is that God gives us what we ourselves have chosen. If I want to be on my own, on my own I shall be. If I do not want God to interfere with my life, God will not interfere; he leaves me utterly alone, and that is the essence of hell.

If the story stopped at this point, the situation would be desperate: by nature we are all spiritually dead, helpless and separated from God. Of course, since we have all gone our own way and turned our backs on God, and since we have frequently disobeyed him and broken his laws, we unquestionably deserve his judgement.

Fortunately that is not the end of the matter. "*But God*", interrupts Paul in two blazing triumphant words, "But God, who is rich in mercy, out of the great love with which he loved us, even when we were dead through our trespasses, made us alive together with Christ (by grace you have been saved)."[13] Entirely through God's love and mercy he offers us in Jesus Christ three things.

First, we need no longer be spiritually dead but can become alive in Christ. The living God, the Creator of all that exists, can become a reality in our own personal experience. We can know God as a Father, we can experience Jesus as our Friend. A journalist said to me in a letter, "It is really wonderful to feel alive with Christ."

Second, we need no longer be separated from God, but can become personally related with him in a glorious intimate relationship that not even death can destroy. And this reconciliation has been made possible for one reason only: the death of Jesus Christ.

"But now, in union with Christ Jesus, you who used to be far away have been brought near by the death of Christ."[14] Christ has become our Mediator, perfectly representing both parties, God and man, and has borne the full weight of our sin in order to bring us back to God.

Third, we need no longer be helpless, for now we are able to fulfil God's special purpose for us in this world. As soon as a person commits his life to Jesus Christ, the Spirit of God comes to indwell his whole being. In the first chapter of his letter to the Ephesians, Paul prayed that the Christians might understand that the power within them in the person of the Holy Spirit is the very power that raised Jesus from the dead. Paul once despaired of the impossibly high standards that God had set before him: "For even though the desire to do good is in me, I am not able to do it. I don't do the good I want to do; instead, I do the evil that I do not want to do. . . . What an unhappy man I am!" What is the answer to this human predicament? "Thanks be to God, through our Lord Jesus Christ! . . . For the law of the Spirit, which brings us life in union with Christ Jesus, has set me free from the law of sin and death."[15] With the Spirit of God within us, the individual is able to fulfil his God-given role, which would otherwise be totally impossible for him. "If anyone is in Christ, he is a new person altogether." Exactly how this process starts we shall examine more closely later.

[1]Reith lectures, 1967

[2]C. S. Lewis *Poems* (Harcourt, Brace Jovanovich)

[3]*Nihilism* is a philosophy of total skepticism. For a nihilist there is no meaning, no aim, no values, no purpose, no answer to the question Why?

[4]*Existentialism* is a philosophy of blind faith in personal experience. The existentialist goes from the dread of a meaningless existence to the brink of despair; and, having faced the situation, makes a deliberate commitment to a course of action. There are no absolutes. "If it's true for *me*, it's true!" It therefore becomes a philosophy of total self-interest.

[5]Psalm 8:1, 3-4

[6]Isaiah 40:15, 17f, 28

[7]Psalm 8:5-6, 9

[8]Romans 12:2 (J. B. Phillips)

[9]1 John 5:19 (TEV)

[10]2 Corinthians 4:4

[11]John 8:44 (TEV)

[12]Ephesians 2:12

[13]Ephesians 2:4f

[14]Ephesians 2:13 (TEV)

[15]Romans 7:18f, 24f, 8:2 (TEV) See Chapter 7 in this book for a fuller discussion of this point.

4

SUFFERING, HELL AND A GODOFLOVE

A God of love? As soon as anyone begins to speak about the existence of a loving, heavenly Father, two huge problems are raised: the suffering of man, and the judgement of God. If there were no loving God, then of course there would not be problems. This is the reason why some of the other religions have no great difficulties with the question of suffering: they do not begin with the concept of a loving God.

It is important, however, to see the logical implications of all this. If there were no God of love, then there would be no justice in the universe, no fairness, no ultimate control. The world would be in chaos, one grotesque meaningless muddle. If I shut my eyes, I am left with darkness. And if I shut my eyes to an infinite personal loving God, of course I am left with darkness, a hopeless situation and a meaningless existence. The early Christians knew only too well that if they closed their eyes to the existence of God, to life after death, to the resurrection of Christ, to heaven and hell, to the justice of God and the vindication of right over wrong, then the world would become one impossible mess: "If our hope in Christ is good for this life only, and no more, then we deserve more pity than anyone else in all the world."[1]

On the other hand, if we accept the existence of a loving God, then how can we reconcile this with the exceedingly ugly fact of suffering? How can we account for Christ's teaching on judgement and hell? "To what divine purpose and in what loving brain was a scorpion forged? What holy chastening is intended when babies are born deformed in mind or body? Is it God's will that two-thirds of the world's population are undernourished? . . . Any hospital will show a gallery of pain which is almost unbearable to the viewers. . . . If there is a God, he is responsible."[2]

Two truths must be kept in mind from the start. First, there is certainly no slick answer to the problem of suffering. Anyone who has witnessed the horrifying scenes of starvation, or cared for those suffering from cancer, leukemia, multiple sclerosis, or mental illness, will not mouth pious clichés. Most of us will be faced with the huge, unanswerable question "Why?" all too often.

Second, we have to admit that a great deal of suffering is caused directly by ourselves. "Where do all the fights and quarrels among you come from? They come from your passions, which are constantly fighting within your bodies. You want things, but you cannot have them, so you are ready to kill; you covet things, but you cannot get them, so you quarrel and fight?"[3] In the vast majority of cases we need to look no further for the cause of suffering than the greed, lust, pride, jealousy, resentment, and selfishness that is in the heart of man. As C. S. Lewis wrote in *The Problem of*

Pain. "It is men, not God, who have produced racks, whips, prisons, slavery, guns, bayonets and bombs; it is by human avarice or human stupidity . . . that we have poverty and overwork. But there remains, nonetheless, much suffering which cannot thus be traced to ourselves. Even if all suffering were man-made, we should like to know the reason for the enormous permission to torture their fellows which God gives to the worst of men."[4] This is the dilemma which we cannot escape. What, then, can we say about suffering?

Our whole approach must be right. If God is God, we could never understand all his ways and works. If we could, God would be no bigger than our minds, and therefore not worth believing in. To say, "I do not know why there is all this suffering" does not mean that there is no reason; but that, as a human being, there is a limit to my understanding; which is true on countless issues. It would be arrogant to say, "Because I do not know of any reason, therefore there is no reason."

This, of course, is the message that comes to us so powerfully through the book of Job. God does not have to justify his existence to us. And if I say to God "First give me satisfactory answers to my questions before I am prepared to consider believing in you," my whole attitude is fundamentally wrong. Several times in the Scriptures we are told that "God opposes the proud, but gives grace to the humble."[5] Until we are prepared to humble ourselves before God, he has nothing for us at all! Our whole attitude therefore must be one of humble, honest inquiry.

Suffering is ultimately due to man's rebellion against God, although on many occasions we may not be able to trace the direct links. We have already seen that often we can; but what about earthquakes, floods, and tornadoes? Surely we must blame God for these? I do not know of any simple answer to this problem, although today, of course, man is hardly in a position to blame the God of the environment, when man's pollution is so appalling on every side. However, the Bible certainly implies that creation itself is corrupted and polluted; and this is directly or indirectly due to the corruption and pollution of man. Since man was given the responsibility of looking after God's world, when man fell, creation fell. It is simply avoiding our own responsibility and guilt if we choose God as a convenient scapegoat.

It is frequently true that it is not so much our situation but the way that we react to it that counts. I talked with two young fathers within a period of about four months. Both had tragically lost their children of four or five. One had died of leukemia; the other had been drowned in a swimming pool. One father had been a professing Christian but was now, because of the experience, a militant atheist. The other father had been a humanist and was now, as a result of the experience, almost a Christian. Here were two very similar tragic experiences but with totally different reactions to each situation.

These reactions are tremendously important. If I become bitter and resentful in my suffering, I still have my suffering, but on top of that I have to contend with my bitterness and resentment as well; and this may be even worse than my initial suffering. Certainly it is worse for other people, and I am responsible for that. On the other hand, if in my suffering I open my heart to the love and comfort and friendship of Jesus Christ, he will wonderfully transform the entire situation—a fact which I see in my pastoral ministry virtually every week of my life.

Those who know the most of the love of God have also known the most suffering. This may be a curious fact, but suffering can produce depth of character, understanding, and spiritual experience, providing we react to it in the right way. Suffering is not always a total disaster.

Richard Wurmbrand, the Rumanian pastor who spent 14 years in a communist prison, including three years in solitary confinement, was able later to say this, "We prisoners have experienced the power of God, the love of God which made us leap with joy. Prison has proved that love is as strong as death. We have conquered through Christ. Officers with rubber truncheons came to interrogate us; we interrogated them, and they became Christians. Other prisoners had been converted. . . . The Communists believe that happiness comes from material satisfaction; but alone in my cell, cold, hungry and in rags, I danced for joy every night. . . . Sometimes I was so filled with joy that I felt I would burst if I did not give it expression. . . . I had discovered a beauty in Christ which I had not known before."[6] Wurmbrand learned the truth of Jesus' promise: "Blessed are you . . . ."[7]

It is often through suffering that God speaks most directly. Naturally we all tend to be independent and self-sufficient and sometimes it is only through suffering that we begin to see our spiritual bankruptcy and start asking the really important questions in life, particularly concerning the purpose of our existence and our relationship with God. Indeed, many of our problems come when we put ourselves at the centre of our universe; and God, if he exists at all, is simply around somewhere to come at our call. All too often we assume that his job is to answer our needs, to give us our rights, and to make sure that everyone has a fair deal. Do you see what we are doing? We are treating God as our servant! Providing he does his job well, we are pleased with him, but if he should fail to serve me or one of my fellow men as I wish, then he is in trouble! We start to criticize him and blame him for his failures. And the common attitude towards God is to keep him standing outside the door until we make a mess of things. Then we decide to call him in to clear up the mess, only to send him out again once things are in order.

What we so often fail to realize is that we are not at the center of the universe: God is! God does not exist for the sake of man, but man exists for the sake of God. "For you created all things, and by your will they were given existence and life."[8]

Further, if we start talking about rights, the only right we have is to be judged by him. We have been created by him, yet have rebelled against him. Therefore the primary question is not "How can God allow suffering?" but "How can God allow sinners into his presence at all?" How is it possible for us to experience his love and forgiveness and peace at all? How is it possible that an infinite holy God should be concerned with us at all? Those are the really difficult questions and it is sometimes only through suffering that we begin to think deeply about these vital issues.

Jesus warned us again and again not to build our hopes

and happiness on this world. Now in this world it is possible to experience a quality of life in Jesus Christ which is so rich and satisfying that the New Testament writers had to speak in superlatives: we read of a fullness of life, a love which surpasses knowledge, a peace which passes all understanding, inexpressible joy. Such phrases imply that no words can sufficiently describe the results of a rich relationship with God. Yet the New Testament writers knew, often in their own painful personal experience, that we are still living in a world full of suffering.

Unlike the prophets of Utopia, Jesus said that "nation will rise against nation, and kingdom against kingdom, and there will be famines and earthquakes in various places: all this is but the beginning of the sufferings."[9] And one day, of course, we must lose everything that is of this world; so that it is our eternal relationship with God that is of ultimate importance.

The disciples once came to Jesus and asked him about the whole question of "innocent suffering." Two thousand Jews had been crucified by the Romans in Galilee; a tower had fallen and had killed eighteen innocent people. "Why does God allow it?" was their obvious question. Jesus did not tackle the philosophical question of suffering, but brought the matter straight back to a practical challenge: "Do you think that these Galileans were worse sinners than all the other Galileans, because they suffered thus? I tell you, no; but unless you repent you will all likewise perish. Or those eighteen upon whom the tower in Siloam fell and killed them, do you think that they were worse offenders than all the others that dwelt in Jerusalem? I tell you no; but unless you repent you will all likewise perish."[10]

God therefore sometimes allows disasters to happen, partly to bring us to our senses. If we all knew that we had 70 years of life, many of us would be unbearably selfish and self-centred for 69 years 364 days, and then we would conveniently repent and expect to said into heaven! But the point is that we do not know about tomorrow. Life is desperately uncertain and sometimes extremely short. We may have to meet our Creator and Judge at any moment. Therefore God, in his love, warns us. He speaks to us through his word and in our conscience. Sometimes he has to speak more loudly through suffering, whether ours or someone else's.

Now you may feel that it is a low motive if we turn to God only when we are crying out for help or when we are afraid of the judgement to come. So it is! It is a very selfish motive indeed if we turn to him as a last resort, like clutching at a straw. But it is part of what C. S. Lewis calls "the divine humility" that God is willing to accept us even on those terms. "If God were proud, he would hardly have us on such terms; but he is not proud, he stoops to conquer, he will have us even though we have shown that we prefer everything else to him, and come to him because there is 'nothing better' to be had. The same humility is shown by all those divine appeals to our fears which trouble high-minded readers of Scripture. It is hardly complimentary to God that we should choose him as an alternative to hell; yet even this he accepts. The creature's illusion of self-sufficiency must, for the creature's sake, be shattered."[11]

The judgement of God

If God is a God of love, how can there possibly be a future judgement and hell?

In one sense it is hard to understand why some people get so upset by the concept of judgement. The necessity of judgement or accountability is built into our whole framework of life. All of us have to give an account of our time, work, money, or abilities to someone sometime. What is so strange, then, that a created being should one day have to give an account of his life to his Creator? People everywhere today are clamoring for justice: justice with wage claims, justice with respect to racial discrimination, justice for the Third World. Fair enough! We should be very much concerned about these things. But God also demands justice. If we are concerned about justice, how much more is God! There could be no goodness nor love of God without justice and judgement. And if there were no justice, we should be left with a terrifying meaninglessness of life.

The Psalmist in Psalm 73 is taken up with this age-old problem: why do the righteous suffer and the wicked prosper? He starts off with a bare statement of faith, but clearly finds it hard to be convinced about it: "Truly God is good to the upright, to those who are pure in heart." He then goes straight on to present his deep-felt problem; "But as for me, my feet had almost stumbled, my steps had well nigh slipped. For I was envious of the arrogant, when I saw the prosperity of the wicked. For they have no pangs; their bodies are sound and sleek. . . . Behold these are the wicked; always at ease, they increase in riches."

The Psalmist then considers his own personal sufferings in spite of his dedication to God: "All in vain have I kept my heart clean and washed my hands in innocence. For all the day long I have been stricken, and chastened every morning. . . . But when I thought how to understand this, it seemed to me a wearisome task." In other words he could not conceive how God could be so monstrously unfair, apparently ignoring his own faith and devotion. At least the perplexity seemed insoluble *"until* I went into the sanctuary of God; then I perceived their end. . . . How they are destroyed in a moment, swept away utterly by terrors! . . . My flesh and my heart may fail, but God is the strength of my heart and my portion for ever. For lo, those who are far from thee shall perish; thou dost put an end to those who are false to thee."

What the Psalmist is saying here is that the mystery of suffering for him was solved when he saw the present "unfairness" of God in the light of eternity. Once the concept of judgement is included, then indeed there will be vindication of right over wrong, and the problem of injustice becomes less perplexing. Certainly it is because we are living in a world full of suffering and sin and evil and violence and lust and greed that God demands the necessity of justice.

However, as soon as anyone talks about the fact of judgement or the possibility of hell, all sorts of objections are raised.

Psychological objections to hell. "Christ's teaching on judgement and hell produces fear and feelings of guilt. These are unhealthy; and it is bad psychology." Sometimes in my ministry I hear a distraught mother shouting terrible threats to her unruly children. Is this bad psychology? Yes it is, because these are, I hope, empty threats. There is nothing good to be said about that. But supposing a mother says to a small child, "Don't run out into the road; you might get run over. Don't go near that fire, you might get burnt." Is that bad psychology? No! these are healthy and realistic warnings; these tragedies could easily happen. I hope that my son has a healthy fear of fire after he plunged both his hands on to the bars of an electric fire only seconds after it had been turned off. Fear is a very healthy emotion. Phobias are unhealthy, but "the fear of the Lord is the beginning of wisdom."

Therefore when Christ warns us repeatedly of the danger of judgement and hell, is this bad psychology? No! These are wise, healthy and realistic warnings. These tragedies could easily happen.

Moral objections to hell. "Hell is unfair! We have all sinned, and it is unfair that some should spend eternity in heaven whilst others spend eternity in hell, just because of a personal belief in Christ. Surely if anyone is decent, honest, kind and generous, that is all that God could possibly require. In fact, many unbelievers are far nicer than many believers!" I hope that no one would dispute that.

However, the nature of God's judgement is to underline the decision that we make *about him*. That is not unfair. Indeed it is important to understand exactly what we mean by sin. Sin is described in the Bible by at least five different Greek words:

Missing the mark.[12] It is a word used in archery when the arrow falls short of the target. Sin is therefore the failure to be what we might have been, and could have been. It means falling short of God's purposes and of God's standard for our life. Perhaps the most basic concept of sin is that we live in God's world without reference to God; we use God's gifts without reference to the Giver. We break the first and great commandment. The greatest commandment is to love God with all our being. The second great commandment is to love other people as ourselves. Now, if we do not love God with all that we have, and if we do not love other people as we should, we have missed the mark. Of course, some people are better than others, humanly speaking. But even though one person might be on the top of Mount Everest in terms of human goodness, while another person is at the bottom of the lowest valley, neither of them can touch the stars. Both have fallen far short of God's perfect standards shown to us in Jesus Christ. Paul once said, "For there is no distinction; since all have sinned and fall short of the glory of God."[13]

Stepping across a line.[14] Since God has made us, he has given us the Maker's Instructions, seen especially in the Ten Commandments. These are not irrelevant and out of date. They form a clear dividing line between what is right and what is wrong, at least in terms of basic principles; and they are designed for our highest good. If I buy some very complicated piece of machinery, I am free to ignore the maker's instructions if I want to; but I am not free to escape the consequences. Further, God's instructions tell us that not only should our relationship with him be right, but that our relationships with other people should also be right, including our family relationships, our sex relationships, and our behavior in society. We are to treat one another with respect, love, honesty and unselfishness. If then I fail to fulfill these instructions, I am guilty of sin. Some might protest that they did not know God's standards, but they still have their own standards as is seen by the way in which they criticize and judge other people. Because of this we cannot escape the righteous judgement of God: "Do you, my friend, pass judgement on others? You have no excuse at all, whoever you are. For when you judge others, but do the same things that they do, you condemn yourself. We know that God is right when he judges the people who do such these. But you, my friend, do these very things yourself for which you pass judgement in others! Do you think you will escape God's judgement?"[15]

Slipping across a line.[16] This implies something not quite so deliberate as the last word, which describes a conscious stepping across a barrier; but because we are naturally sinful we have a bias towards sin. Sometimes in conversation we make a remark that is biting or cutting; it hurts. Later we are often sorry that we have said it, but "it just slipped out." That is what we are like.

Lawlessness or *rebellion.*[17] I go my way, not God's way; I do what I want, not what God wants. It is a fundamentally wrong attitude towards God: "I will not have this man to reign over me!" This, of course, is the really hateful part of sin: when God has given me everything that I possess, life and breath and all things, when God loves me and wants me to know his love and peace and forgiveness, when God has given me his own son Jesus Christ to be my Friend and Savior, if then I turn my back on God, and say, in effect, "Stop interfering!", then that rebellion is sin.

Debt.[18] The word refers to sins of omission, which are perhaps the most devastating of all. I once came across these words in a little tract: "I never was guilty of wrong actions. But on my account lives have been lost, trains have been wrecked, ships have gone down at sea, cities have burned, battles have been lost, and governments have failed. I never struck a blow nor spoke an unkind word, but because of me homes have been broken up, friends have grown cold, the laughter of children has ceased, wives have shed bitter tears, brothers and sisters have forgotten, and fathers and mothers have gone broken-hearted to their graves. Who am I? I am *neglect.*" We do not have to be against God to be in danger of judgement. We simply have to neglect his offer of life in Jesus Christ. That is another side of the nature of sin. And if, in effect, I say to God now, "Depart from me," is it unfair that God should one day reply, "Depart from *me*: it was your decision, not mine." This is the essence of judgement: God gives us what we ourselves have chosen.

Indeed, if it is a case of being unfair at all, we could well say that forgiveness and mercy were unfair, undeserved. Why should God bother? Why should God forgive? Why should Christ die on the cross in our place? These are the really hard questions to answer. "To many moderns, that God can punish seems to need explanation. To the early Christians, that God could forgive was the amazing thing."[19]

Theological objections to hell. "I believe in a God of love; I don't believe that he would condemn anyone."

However, as soon as we turn to God's self-revelation in the Scriptures, we may find two surprises. The first surprise is that there is hardly anything about hell in the Old Testament. Some think of the God of the Old Testament as harsh and severe, but in fact there is very little teaching about his final judgement. The second surprise is that there is not much teaching on hell in the epistles of the New Testament. Therefore it is not a corruption of the Gospel by Peter or Paul or John. Indeed, if we want to learn about judgement and hell, we need to turn to the teachings of Jesus himself. And it is a remarkable fact that Jesus, who more than anyone showed us the love of God, also told us more than anyone of the judgement of God. The theologian Jeremias once wrote, "The message of Jesus is not only the proclamation of salvation, but also the announcement of judgement, a cry of warning, and a call to repentance in view of the terrible urgency of the crises. The number of parables in this category is nothing less than awe-inspiring."[20]

Why did Jesus of all people speak in such solemn terms? Partly, I believe, because the teaching is so severe that we might not take it except from someone who so manifestly loved and cared for us. Partly also, because in his love and care Jesus spoke frankly about our greatest need, and did something about it at the cost of his own life. If I find someone lying in the road with a broken leg, what love do I show him if I simply say, "I see your shoelace is undone; let me tie it for you", and then walk off! True love will always care about the deepest and most urgent needs, and do something about them.

I do not believe that we shall ever understand the

wonder of God's love except in the context of judgement. Perhaps the greatest love verse in the Bible is John 3.16, "For God so loved the world that he gave his only Son, that whoever believes in him *should not perish* but have eternal life." The astonishing measure of God's love is that we all deserve to perish, because we have broken his laws so 9ften. But he so loved the world, including you and me, that we need not perish but find in his Son eternal life. God knows that naturally we are all going down a broad road which leads to destruction. In his love he sets before us one obstacle after another to stop us going along that road. He gives us the Bible, Christian books, Christian friends, Christian churches, and above all the outstretched arms of Jesus on the cross. If I choose to run past all those obstacles, then I have only myself to blame for the consequences. It is part of the essence and tragedy of love that it risks being rejected. It is simply shallow thinking to say that the judgement of God is inconsistent with the love of God. It is because God loves that he will not force, and therefore there is the terrifying possibility of rejecting and forfeiting his love. If I choose to do that, I have automatically chosen his judgement instead. If I do not want God, I do not have God. If I want to be on my own, I shall be on my own. This is the first principle of hell. It is perfectly fair, and quite consistent with a God of love.

What will be the criterion of judgement? Christ made it clear that judgement would always be according to opportunity. Those who have never heard about Christ can still know something about God through creation, and conscience. They will therefore be judged by the moral judgements that they have made about other people, for by these judgements they show they clearly have some sense of right and wrong. Again it is perfectly fair. But who has lived up even to his own standards in life, let alone God's? However, as the Swiss theologian René Pache has expressed it, "God does not allow any of his creatures to be eternally lost, without, in his own way, seeking to win them. Thus when the time comes to leave the world, every man has had enough light to have accepted or rejected God, so that he is fully responsible to him."

For those who have heard about Christ, the position is quite clear. We shall be judged according to our response to Christ and our relationship with him. What have we done with God's Son? What place have we given to God's greatest gift to us? That will be the criterion of judgement; and to many he will have to say "I never knew you, depart from me."[21]

What will be the nature of judgement? The answer, for those who have not responded to Christ, is eternal separation from God and from everything good. And to stress the seriousness of this Christ used one solemn expression after another. Further, when we see him weeping over the city of Jerusalem because of its coming judgement, and when we see Christ's own appalling agony on the cross, it is quite certain that he was not playing with words when he spoke about the horrors of "outer darkness."

Further, if anyone is still baffled to see how suffering and hell are consistent with a God of love, we need to look carefully at God's own revelation in terms of his Son Jesus Christ. Christ not only taught repeatedly that God is a God of love, but he had a perfect relationship of love with his own Father. He spoke often of the Father loving the Son and the Son loving the Father. More than that, he showed the love of God by his immense compassion. He cared for individuals in all their ugliness and need. He had compassion on lepers and outcasts, prostitutes and thieves, the deaf and dumb and blind and lame. He loved Zacchaeus, the cheat whom everybody despised. He cared for the Samaritan woman whom so many had used. He washed the feet of his own disciples. He prayed even for his murderers; and while hanging on the cross, in excruciating pain, he cared for the personal needs of his own mother, and brought peace and forgiveness to one of the thieves crucified with him. Everywhere we see the love of Jesus, or the love of God as expressed in his own Son.

At the same time, everywhere we look in Jesus' life we see suffering too. He was born in poverty, despised and rejected by men, a man of sorrows and acquainted with grief. He was misunderstood, slandered and hated. He knew oppression, loneliness, torture, and the most agonising death reserved for the very worst of criminals. "Surely he has borne our griefs and carried our sorrows; yet we esteemed him stricken, smitten by God, and afflicted. . . . He was oppressed, and he was afflicted, yet he open not his mouth; like a lamb that is led to the slaughter, and like a sheep that before its shearers is dumb, so he opened not his mouth."[22]

William Temple once explained the problem like this, " 'There cannot be a God of love,' men say, 'because if there was, and he looked upon the world, his heart would break.' The church points to the cross and says, 'It did break.' 'It is God who made the world,' men say. 'It is he who should bear the load.' The church points to the cross and says, 'He did bear it.' "

When it comes to the question of judgement and hell, nowhere can the reality of these be seen more clearly than on the cross: "He was wounded for our transgressions, he was bruised for our iniquities; upon him was the chastisement that made us whole, and with his stripes we are healed. All we like sheep have gone astray; we have turned everyone to his own way; and the Lord has laid on him the iniquity of us all."[23] Listen to Jesus's cry of intense suffering, "My God, my God, why have you forsaken me?" The precise significance of these words can be lost in their familiarity. The essence of sin is to forsake God; therefore the consequence of sin is to be God-forsaken. God underlines our decision and gives us what we want. That is the nature of hell: to be God-forsaken. And such is the love of God that his own Son suffered hell on the cross for us, that we might be forgiven and loved and brought to know the love of God in our own sinful, rebellious hearts. That is the supreme demonstration that, even in the midst of suffering and hell, God is a God of love. "In the long run," writes C. S. Lewis, "the answer to all those who object to the doctrine of hell is itself a question: 'What are you asking God to do?' To wipe out their past sins and, at all costs, to give them a fresh start, smoothing every difficulty and offering every miraculous help? But he has done so, on Calvary."[24]

[1] 1 Corinthians 15:19 (TEV)
[2] William Miller, *The God I Want* (Constable), page 52
[3] James 4:1f (TEV)
[4] Op. cit. (Macmillan)
[5] James 4:6; 1 Peter 5:5; Psalm 138:6
[6] *In God's Underground* (Diane Books)
[7] Matt. 5:11
[8] Revelation 4:11 (TEV)
[9] Matthew 24:7f
[10] Luke 13:2-5
[11] *The Problem of Pain* (Macmillan)
[12] Greek: *hamartia*
[13] Romans 3:22-23
[14] Greek: *parabasis*
[15] Romans 2:1-3 (TEV)
[16] Greek: *paraptoma*
[17] Greek: *anomia*
[18] Greek: *opheilema*
[19] Leighton Ford, *The Christian Persuader* (Harper & Row)
[20] Joachim Jeremias, *The Parables of Jesus* (Scribners)
[21] Matthew 7:23
[22] Isaiah 53:4,7
[23] Isaiah 53:5-6
[24] *The Problem of Pain* (Macmillan)

5
THE REVOLUTION OF LOVE

If there is nothing more basic than love, there is nothing more obvious than the revolution of love which has changed so much of society in recent years. At least, that is true of the sex revolution, which dominates the scene today. The question is whether this revolution of sex can rightly be called a revolution of love; and how does it compare with the Christian concept of love, as seen in Jesus Christ.

Much personal counselling today is concerned with relationships that have gone wrong. The major tragedy in terms of relationships is that we so often use one another. We may call it "love"; but it is a travesty of the real meaning of love if I "love" a person for what I can get out of that person. Of course, we would hotly deny that we are doing this. "I really love her," we say; "I would do anything for her!" No doubt that is true, as long as all is going well. But the fact remains that society today is littered with broken relationships, broken promises, broken hearts, broken homes, broken marriages, broken lives and often broken health. Why? Because all too often we *use* people to satisfy our needs. Especially this is true with the revolution of sex.

"Because of the pill," said Dr. Helena Wright, "we are at last able to free human sexual capacities. If a person is capable of responding to three or four partners, that's a rich personality!"[1] This means that I could become a rich personality by *using* three or four different partners. Why not? Perhaps they are *using* me. It is all part of the sex revolution of today.

Of course, there is nothing new in all this. You will find a rampantly permissive society as far back as Genesis 6. And in New Testament times there was an almost total disregard of sexual morality. A Roman Empress in AD 50 was a common prostitute; of the first 15 Roman Emperors, 14 were practicing homosexuals; and Jerome tells us of a woman marrying her 23rd husband, she being his 21st wife!

Within the last century the pendulum in the West has swung from one extreme to the other. Whereas the charge levelled at the Victorians was "love without sex", today it is "sex without love". A modern poet describes physical and emotional experience which is totally devoid of any real relationship:

"The Act of Love lies somewhere
Between the belly and the mind
I lost the love some time ago
Now I've only the act to grind

Brought her back from a party
Don't bother swopping names
Identity's not needed
When you are only playing games

84

High on bedroom darkness
We endure the pantomime
Ships that go bump in the night
Run aground on the sands of time

Saved in the nick of dawn
It's cornflakes and then goodbye
Another notch of the headboard
Another day wondering why

The Act of Love lies somewhere
Between the belly and the mind
I lost the love some time ago
Now I have only the act to grind."[2]

What's wrong? Should we accept a bourgeois morality? Why conform to middle class values? Many young people today are rightly exposing this morality as having no basis for its values, that is, no basis apart from convention. So many are seeing very clearly (and this is perfectly fair), that these standards by themselves, without any solid basis, are arbitrary, traditional or bourgeois. One obvious reaction is to destroy the system. Who cares? Why shouldn't I? What's to stop me? These are perfectly valid questions.

In fact, the only solid answer to these questions is that God has given us standards of behavior which are not arbitrary. They are good and right, and expressions of his love. Because he is a God of love, he has shown us the greatest meaning of love, and the best possible relationship that we can have with one another. Thus we need to look carefully at God's standards in terms of personal relationships, as revealed in the Bible and as taught supremely by Jesus Christ. And if you think that the Bible is anti-sex you are very much mistaken. It sees sex as one of the greatest gifts given to us by our Creator, an expression of his creative work of love, and the most intimate token of love between a man and a woman that they can possibly have. There are many magnificent statements about sex relationships in the Bible, not least in the Song of Solomon, one of the most beautiful love poems that you can find anywhere in ancient literature.

God's standards are definite

In the first place, God's standards are quite definite. There is nothing ambiguous about them, which is why Christ's teaching is so unacceptable and unpopular in certain quarters. Basically there is one clear principle: no *sex outside of marriage*. The biblical standard is chastity before marriage and fidelity after marriage. "Let marriage be held in honor among all, and let the marriage bed be undefiled; for God will judge the immoral and adulterous."[3] Further, Jesus not only endorsed those standards, which go back to Old Testament days; he applied them to our thoughts and imaginations as well as to our actions. "You have heard that it was said, 'You shall not commit adultery.' But I say to you that everyone who looks at a woman lustfully has already committed adultery with her in his heart."[4] This of course hammers the hypocrisy which makes the open and outward behavior so important, regardless of private thoughts and deeds.

God's standards are right and good

In the second place, God's standards are right and

good. God is no spoil-sport! It is not just a matter of Thou shalt not! Thou shalt not! Thou shalt not!" Far from it. God is the Maker of sex, and therefore in its rightful place sex is very beautiful indeed. Jesus once said that eternal life means knowing God, and the word for "knowing" is a word that is quite often used in the Bible in terms of a sexual relationship. This intimate human bond is frequently a picture in the Bible of the deep spiritual bond which an individual can have with his Creator.

Indeed it is precisely because sex is so beautiful that God, the Maker of sex, has given us the Maker's Instructions. And centuries of history have proved that his instructions are absolutely right. The Harvard sociologist, P. A. Sorokin, in his book *The American Sex Revolution,* describes the Russian attitude of the '20s: "The revolution leaders deliberately attempted to destroy marriage and the family. The legal distinction between marriage and casual sexual intercourse was abolished. Bigamy and polygamy were permissible under the new provisions. Abortion was facilitated in the State institutions. Pre-marital relationships were praised; extramarital relationships were considered normal. . . . Within a few years millions of lives, especially of young girls, were wrecked. The hatred and conflicts . . . rapidly mounted and so did psychoneuroses. Work in the nationalized factories slackened. The government was forced to reverse its policy." As a result, Russia has returned to very strict standards of sexual morality.

China, too, is outwardly a clean and moral country, sexually speaking. Further, these atheistic states have not only returned to the Maker's instructions, which they have had to learn the hard way, but they now enforce them in the strongest possible terms. They see a sex revolution as one of the greatest threats for any society. Today's revolutionaries know this, of course. The Yippie leader, Jerry Rubin, once said, "We aim to splinter society by a combination of sex and violence and drugs." In Russia and China pornography is regarded as a sign of the " decadence of the capitalist system."

Moreover, on a personal basis, God really does know what he is talking about in his instructions. A girl I have already referred to told me that she had felt for years "as guilty as hell" because of her free and easy sex experiences. Several couples have come to me with serious problems in their sex relationships within marriage, simply because of their free love experiences outside marriage. Free sex does not increase a person's capacity for love and sex; very much the reverse.

Abortion too presents desperate problems. On my way to a meeting I was handed a Women's Lib. tract called "Enlightenment." It said "Women's Liberation demands control over her own body and her own destiny, free contraceptives and free abortion on demand. . . ." Is this really enlightenment? What is the value of human life and where is the meaning of love if there is free abortion on demand? What is the meaning of life when the first stages of life can be destroyed so readily in the interests of self and sex? We have not even considered all the other attendant problems. According to one report, venereal disease is now the commonest disease apart from the common cold.

When God says, "Save sex for marriage," he is not

trying to frustrate us. He wants us to know the greatest possible joy. A parachutist should not complain of instructions not to jump unless he has put on his parachute. The advice is simply for his own good. He may, of course, decide to jump with no strings attached. He is free to ignore the instructions. He is free to jump if he wants to. But he is not free to escape the consequences.

I know of one girl, and probably there are thousands like her, who told me that she continues to sleep with her boyfriend because she is afraid that otherwise she would lose him. Here is a relationship, supposedly of love, which already is being spoilt by fear and mistrust and uncertainty. There is no firm commitment. And if the moral fence has once been jumped, how can you be sure that it will not happen again? Victor Brown in *A Kind of Loving* said, "To get really free, though, I have to get right away from her, because while I am still with her I have that feeling that I am just about the rottenest devil alive for treating her this way." Such tensions are common among those for whom sex is mere selfishness.

God's standards are not easy

In the third place God's standards are not easy for us. None of the best things in life are easy. Therefore "free love," when referring to sexual relationships, is a contradiction in terms: if it is free, it is not love; if it is love, it is not free. A woman doctor put it like this: "Our thirteen year old can now pass happily from boy to boy with no fear, except the knowledge that it is not love that she is giving or receiving, frustrated that the act of procreation is of her choice, degraded as she knows she is only an article to be used and discarded. The whole gamut of emotions released must be thwarted and stifled—the only reward is orgasm."[5]

Temporary sexual relationships so often mean acting a lie. A person wants the expression of love, in terms of sex, without the reality of love, in terms of responsibilities. If I really love a girl, I must express that love for her by giving my whole life to her, not by giving her or getting from her a few moments of sexual pleasure; nor by agreeing, even mutually, to opt out of the relationship if things become difficult. Real love involves firm commitment. Real love, with any depth, will grow and develop through difficulties in that commitment. The self-control and discipline and forgiveness that are so often needed within a true and lasting relationship are the very factors which develop a really mature and beautiful love relationship. Sex is only a temporary physical expression of the much greater bond of love itself.

I have often been asked "What's wrong with a steady partner, especially if we are probably going to get married some day anyway?" Here it is not a question of promiscuity, with all its serious risks of VD; it is simply premarital intercourse, because, for one reason or another, a marriage is not yet possible or convenient. Therefore why not sleep together, with a steady or serious partner? My answer very briefly is this.

First, even with the Pill, you cannot escape the possibility of pregnancy; and the British Medical Association says that the fear of pregnancy, which is very widespread, is a threat to mental health and academic work. Further, both abortion and unwanted babies present immense problems. There is only one completely safe form of contraception, and it is the cheapest. It is to say *no*!

Second, where there is no binding commitment as in a marriage service, there will nearly always be an element of fear in the relationship—the fear of losing him or her. And fear is the opposite of love.

Third, in sex before marriage there is nearly always a degree of selfishness and greed: "I must have this *now*!" This leads to a lack of self-respect, and I do not know of anyone who later has felt that they have gained by it.

Fourth, although we dress it up in high sounding phrases such as "pre-marital intercourse", Jesus called it fornication and sin. It breaks God's laws, and no one can do that without paying the consequences sooner or later.

This is real love

If we want to understand the real meaning of love, we must look carefully at both the teaching and the life of Jesus Christ. Jesus mixed with the most progressive and permissive society of his day. He was loved by prostitutes and drunkards, yet he himself was absolutely pure. He was "tempted in every way that we are, but did not sin."[6] That is why he was and is so attractive. Let us therefore look more closely at God's love as shown to us in Christ.

Love is concerned with people. Jesus was not in the least concerned about himself and his own selfish desires. He put all that totally on one side. Never once do we find a trace of him using people for his own selfish ends. Always he went out in love and compassion to people as people, individual people, each one vitally important to God. Many of them were not very lovable: traitors and con men, prostitutes and pimps, the social outcasts of his day, the drop-outs and rejects of society, the unwanted and the unloved. Sometimes, too, he came to the rich and influential, the religious and respectable. And he came to everybody with love, friendship, understanding and forgiveness. Indeed, his enemies, intending it as an abuse, called him, "the friend of sinners". But that was and is the most wonderful fact about him. "This is what love is: it is not that we have loved God, but that he loved us and sent his Son to be the means by which our sins are forgiven."[7] Therefore he reaches out to us, whoever we may be or whatever we may have done. If you have made rather a mess of your sex life, Jesus loves you. If you have not made a mess of your sex life, Jesus loves you. If you feel totally unworthy of him, Jesus loves you. If you feel no need of him at all, Jesus loves you. Whatever our actions or attitudes might be, God takes the initiative and reaches out to us in love through his Son Jesus Christ.

That is the most wonderful truth. A friend of mine is a professional actress, attractive, loving, and a beautiful personality. She must have had many friends all her life. Not long ago she found Jesus as her personal Friend and she said that she has never experienced such love before in her life.

This personal love of Jesus for individuals is, of course, very striking. You may follow the teachings of Karl Marx, Buddha, Bertrand Russell, Guru Maharaj Ji, Sun Myung Moon, or anyone else that you might mention. Not one of those individuals could love you personally. Many of them are dead anyway. But you can know the love of the living Jesus in your own personal experience.

Love satisfies the deepest needs of people. It is not content with superficial problems; it tackles the real problems and satisfies the depths of our being. One of the tragedies of human relationships, especially as seen in terms of sex, is that these cannot possibly satisfy in any complete or lasting way. The really deep needs for forgiveness, purpose, peace, go completely unfulfilled. With human love, we are always wanting more and more and more. Jesus once said to a woman well-known in Samaria for her popularity with men, "You'll thirst again!" In other words you will never satisfy your deepest thirst from your outside world, because your inside world is empty and dry, crying out for peace and for love. Sex will never give a person that. If anything it will make our deepest thirst more acute than ever before: "You will thirst again!" "But," said Jesus, "whoever drinks the water that I shall give him will never thirst; the water that I shall give him will become in him a spring of water welling up to eternal life."[8]

Love is willing for sacrifice. Jesus made that quite clear, both by his teaching and by his example. He told us to forgive and forgive and forgive—seventy times seven. He told us to love our enemies and to pray for those who make life difficult for us, to give without any hope of return, and to get involved with the needs of people. It is one thing to get involved in *causes* (an easy alternative); but it is quite another thing to get involved with *people*, needy and demanding people.

Someone has described the sort of love which is common today like this: "I was hungry and you formed a committee to investigate my hunger. I was homeless and you filed a report of my plight. I was sick and you held a seminar on the situation of the underprivileged. You have investigated all aspects of my plight; and yet I am still hungry, homeless and sick."

Not so Jesus! So great was his love for people that he himself was often hungry and homeless, tired and lonely. He prayed for his enemies, and he gave himself continually to bring his love to men and women and children with all their complicated needs. He even gave his life, on the cross, to take away our sins. And there on the cross all our sin, guilt and filth was taken by Jesus so that every single one of us can know God's forgiveness and peace. That is the measure of his love.

It is so easy talking about the cross. But try to imagine Jesus—the loveliest man that ever lived, gentle and compassionate, strong, honest and true—being crucified for your sins.

Certainly there was *physical* pain. Jesus was whipped with leather thongs to which sharp pieces of metal or bone had been fastened, ripping his flesh. Many victims died from this scourging alone. He staggered on the road, carrying the instrument of his execution; and when he was held down on the cross, huge nails and spikes were driven through the palms of his hands and his feet. The cross was then lifted up and dropped into the hole prepared for it. There Jesus hung, with the heat, thirst, flies and gnats, and searing, stabbing pain shooting through every nerve of his body. It was excruciatingly painful.

On top of that Jesus experienced emotional agony. After all, he had come to love people with a degree and intensity of love that we have never experienced. What happened? They mocked him, despised him, rejected him and crucified him. Think, for a moment, of the person you love most of all in this world. Imagine your feelings if that person mocked you, despised, rejected and crucified you! If you can imagine such an appalling thing, you will have a glimpse of the mental sufferings of Jesus when he died for your sins.

Worst of all was the *spiritual* torment, as he took the full weight and penalty of our sins upon himself that we might be free to know God's love. How could we ever fully understand the horror of that spiritual alienation from God that Jesus experienced when he cried out "My God, my God, why have you forsaken me?" But, in a word, it was hell—total spiritual anguish, in order that *we* might forever enjoy the peace and freedom of God's gracious presence. Peter once said, "Christ also died for sins once for all, the righteous for the unrighteous, that he might bring us to God."[9] Paul wrote, "God shows his love for us in that while we were yet sinners Christ died for us."[10]

In the fourth place, *love requires a response.* Love always does! When I proposed to that lovely girl who has now become my wife, I said "Will you?" I was expecting an answer, yes or no. It might have been "wait," but that is a risky response. There may not be another opportunity! When, therefore, Jesus says "Will you?" offering you both himself and his love, it is a terribly important moment. We are told in the Bible to "seek the Lord while he may be found, call upon him while he is near."[11] There are certain moments in a person's life when God is especially to be found, and he is very near. He waits for our response. He will not force us, because he loves us. We are quite free to ignore him or to reject him. But we are not free to escape the consequences. Therefore, in his love he is urgent.

Having known the reality of the love of Jesus in my own life for many years, and having seen this revolution of love taking place in the lives of hundreds and thousands of people whom I have personally met or known, I can never, never understand why some people do not want to get involved. There is nothing so beautiful or totally satisfying as the love of Jesus. It is always fresh and new, and it is a love which never fails.

[1] *Sunday Telegraph,* 30 November 1969
[2] © Roger McGough 1967
[3] Hebrews 13:4
[4] Matthew 5:27f
[5] *Pornography, The Longford Report,* page 76
[6] Hebrews 4:15 (TEV)
[7] 1 John 4:10 (TEV)
[8] John 4:14

b

DEATH
AND THE
OCCULT

What happens at death? It is the one question we cannot escape, because death is the one event that we must all face. George Bernard Shaw once wrote in characteristic fashion, "Death is the ultimate statistic: one out of one dies." What happens at death? Job asked 3,000 years ago, "If a man dies, shall he live again?" Tennyson longed for "the touch of a vanished hand and the sound of a voice that is still".

Today, in spite of all our progress, most people are thoroughly confused about death. Usually there is an astonishing silence about this subject. Fifty years ago everyone talked realistically about death, but no one talked about sex. Today everyone talks about sex, but very few talk about death, unless they have to; and then so often they do it in veiled clichés. Indeed, we fight death for all we are worth, with pills and prescriptions, transplants and treatments and life-sustaining mechanisms and just in case the "worst" should happen, there are of course insurance policies and pension plans. "If you had died yesterday, what would you be worth today?" asks an advertisement, a thought-provoking question. It was, in fact, put out by an insurance company, urging you to make your death worthwhile for at least someone!

A few years ago, talk-show host David Frost devoted one of his programs to the theme of death. A panel of celebrities had been arranged, and each was asked to state his views. In many ways it was a most unsatisfactory program, but at least two things emerged; there was almost total confusion and haziness about death. "I think that possibly, perhaps, or maybe . . ." No one had any clear ideas. And it was obvious that almost everyone was frightened of death. Indeed, someone has said that "the fear of death is so natural that all life is one long effort not to think about it".

That is no doubt why it is one of the non-topics of conversation today. Apart from the Christian faith, there are no real answers at all in the face of death. Therefore the vast majority of people are afraid to die: not perhaps when they are discussing it in a detached way, sitting comfortably in an armchair and talking pleasantly with their friends; but when face to face with man's final enemy most people deep down are afraid.

A young writer once expressed it like this:
'I lie awake worrying what it will be like to be dead.
I lie awake worrying how dark will the coffin be.
I lie awake and feel how cold my life will be.
It makes no sense the end of life being death.
Just a memory, and then nothing,
Absolutely nothing, just nothing.
Death is like a black hole without any sides.
Death is like a thought without a thinker.
Death is fear. . . .'

98

What causes this fear at death? It is primarily the fear of the unknown. At death we are cut off from the world that we know and the people that we love. "We brought nothing into this world, and it is certain that we carry nothing out." We leave behind our home, our family, our friends, our possessions—everything. We are deposited alone, without luggage, in the great unknown.

What happens at death? The answer to that question affects not only our death but the whole of our life. Carl Jung once wrote, "The question of the meaning and the worth of life never becomes more urgent or more agonizing than when we see the final breath leave a body which a moment before was living." An extraordinary comment! The urgent questions about life come at death! Here is a body that has just died. What is different? It all looks remarkably the same. Philosophers have always maintained that the key to life is to be found in coming to terms with death. No man can live well until he can die well, for he might be living in a fool's paradise. I once talked with a medical student who had just dissected his first human body. The corpse had been there in front of him, and he had cut away different parts of the anatomy. It was like a wax model. "If this is all that we become at death, what is the point of anything?" he asked. Has life any ultimate purpose? Or is it in the last analysis, earth to earth, ashes to ashes, dust to dust? What happens at death?

There are, of course, many theories, and we need to look at a few of them briefly.

Certainly **atheism** has no answer. The atheist says

categorically, "Nothing happens after death". In some famous words of Bertrand Russell, in his book *Why I am not a Christian,* "When I die I shall rot, and nothing of my ego will survive. . . . There is darkness without and when I die there will be darkness within. There is no splendor, no vastness anywhere: only triviality for a moment, and then nothing." In many ways this is an appalling philosophy. If when a person dies, he must say to those whom he loves "I shall never see you again"; if he just rots in the grave; if there is no heaven, no vindication of right over wrong, no hope whatever concerning the future, this is not only a philosophy of total despair, but it makes nonsense of any true purpose in life.

If that were true, why bother about anything at all? "One day I, too, will be dead and snow will fall on my tomb, while the living will laugh, embrace and enjoy life. I shall be unable to participate in their joys; I shall not even know them. I will simply not exist any more. After a short time no one will remember me. So what use is anything?"[1]

It is important to realize, however, that the atheist's view is pure theory. He has no clear evidence to support it. Indeed, as we shall see in a moment, all the solid, substantial, historical evidence is against him, in particular the person and teaching and resurrection of Jesus Christ.

Second, **mysticism** has no answers. In an interview with the Maharishi Mahesh Yogi, of Beatle fame, the interviewer, Dennis Hart, tried to find out about the Maharishi's Master, Guru Dev. "Where is he now?" he asked a teacher. "Well, he died." "Yes, I know, but where is he now?" He was told, "That is a philosophical and theosophical question I am not qualified to answer".

Not satisfied he tried again, asking the Maharishi's closest lieutenant, Max Fisher, once a lecturer in London: "Where is Guru Dev now?" "Maharishi never speaks about that. Maharishi has got rid of all belief. By now I have had enough glimpses of myself (which is universal) to be able to ignore the question of the cessation of a limited self-hood. Those glimpses are so powerful that they may take over the whole of your life, and you feel identified with that universal self-hood."

Understandably not satisfied, the interviewer asked the Maharishi himself: "Where is Guru Dev, now that he is dead?" Impersonally the answer came, "When the boundaries relax, what remains is the boundless."

What does all that mean? What is the evidence for it? What hope does it give to a man who is dying? What comfort can it bring to those who are bereaved? It is fairly obvious that the mystic has no real answer when confronted with death.

Third, **universalism** gives no true answer, though it attractively suggests that everyone is welcomed into heaven, regardless of his response to God the Father or God the Son during his life-time. It might be comforting to believe this, but there are various problems with this theory. It makes nonsense of heaven, if heaven were full of those who wanted to have nothing to do with God when they were here on earth: Hitlers, Satanists and all the God-haters down the ages. It also makes nonsense of man's freedom: if we are free now to reject God's love, but one day forced to accept it, then what is the meaning of our freedom? Then it makes nonsense of the person and teaching of Jesus Christ. Jesus taught so clearly that there would one day be a judgement to come, when we should be either eternally with God or eternally separated from God. If that were not true, then the warnings of Jesus would become dishonest attempts to frighten us into faith. "He becomes like the very worst sort of school teacher who, having failed to make his subject intrinsically attractive, and being without any personal charm to make up for this deficiency, resorts to threats, which at last he lacks the strength of character to enforce."[2] Everything about Christ, his love and humility and honesty and integrity, utterly discounts that theory.

Fourth, **reincarnation** is no answer. For some it may seem to be an attractive theory, although I am not sure that everyone wants to reappear on this earth, and finally lose his identity by being absorbed into some universal consciousness! But the main argument against reincarnation is that it is contrary to the teaching of Christ. Repeatedly he made it clear that at death there would be a great separation between those who know Christ and those who do not. After that it will be impossible to change sides. In Luke 16.19ff Jesus spoke about two men who died, one who went to heaven and the other who went to hell. The one in hell now realized his tragic mistake throughout his life, and cried out for mercy. But he was told that between heaven and hell there was "a great chasm fixed in order that those who would pass from here to you may not be able, and none may cross from there to us."

The Bible is totally silent about any possibility of rein-carnation, and there is no evidence for any second chance after death. Indeed the positive teaching is that "It is appointed for men to die once and after that comes judgement".[3]

Fifth, **spiritualism** has no answers in the face of death. It is understandable why some turn to spiritu-alism, especially after the death of a friend or relative whom they have loved, and sometimes comforting messages are received. What can we say about this?

The occult
We need to look for a moment at the whole question of the occult. The word means *secret* or *dark* or *mysteri-ous*, something which transcends our ordinary world of five senses. Although there is a huge variety of oc-cult practices, they can be divided into three main sections. First there is *fortune telling,* such as astrology, palmistry, clairvoyance, divination, rod and pendu-lum, color therapy, and radiesthesia. All forms of for-tune telling are increasingly popular today, with books on astrology booming and horoscopes to be found everywhere. In the U. S. there are 1,750 daily news-papers; and in 1,200 you will find a daily horoscope. In Paris, according to *Time* magazine, there is one priest for every 5,000, one doctor for every 514, and one spiritist for every 120.

Then there is *magic* which involves the manipula-tion of supernatural powers for various purposes, such as charms or curses. Although there is a distinc-tion between black and white magic, both come under the overall heading of the occult.

There is also *spiritism* or spirit-communication, such as table lifting, glass moving, ouija boards, and automatic writing.

It is worth noting that the principles and practices of occultism are the same today as they were 5,000 years ago. Yet in this sophisticated space-age, it is becoming more and more popular. In recent years Britain has become the world center of occultism, and Americans have organized "psychic" package tours to London. Witchcraft has also developed considerably, and according to various reports there are several thousand practicing witches in Great Britain alone.

Why do we find this astonishing resurgence of occult practice in an age of science and technology? Partly it is because no one, apart from Jesus Christ and the Christian faith, has any solid answers at all in the face of death. Further, most people are hungry for God or for some sort of spiritual reality, because God has made them that way. Materialism does not satisfy, and cannot answer the vital questions of life. However, sometimes the Church, in its formal traditional establishment, has appeared irrelevant and remote. Two students once explained to me why they had turned to spiritualism. They complained that they had been to many religious meetings in churches, but always it had been words, words, words. They were now sick of words, and they were seriously searching for spiritual reality. They claimed that they had found this reality at a seance.

What can we say of the dangers of occultism? Some phenomena, of course, may be spurious and easily explained away, but much of it is both real and dangerous. One of the leading spiritists in America said that he did not know a single case of spiritism where there had not been *distinct deterioration* of physical, mental or spiritual faculties.

One minister tried to discredit occult practices as mere superstition, and paid a large sum for a sophisticated horoscope in order to prove that it did not work. For eight years he became increasingly disturbed as its predictions were fulfilled. He found it hard to pray, and worship and Bible reading became increasingly difficult. He came to the conclusion that he had placed himself under some occult and evil power. Finally he renounced the horoscope and asked God's forgiveness for having dabbled with the occult. From that moment onwards, the horoscope became inaccurate for him. His personal experience of God was restored.

A friend of mine was called in to help five students who had only recently started playing with a ouija board. Although to begin with it was no more than a party game, they soon experienced a series of strange and frightening events. One of the girls became violent and even tried to kill another member of the group. Soon they were seriously affected both mentally and physically, and for three weeks were unable to attend their college classes. Later they were all set free by the power of Jesus Christ, but it had been a most distressing experience.

The evidence is that any person who dabbles in the occult is playing with something dangerous and destructive, which can lead to tragic situations, and from which there is no final deliverance, except through the power of Christ. We should not be surprised by this, because there are almost 50 references to the occult in the Bible and every time it is described as being thoroughly evil and offensive to God. "There shall not be found among you anyone who burns his son or his daughter as an offering, anyone who practices divination, a soothsayer, or an augur, or a sorcerer, or a charmer, or a medium, or a wizard, or a necromancer [= spiritualist]. For whoever does these things is an abomination to the Lord; and because of these abominable practices the Lord your God is driving them out before you. . . . For these nations, which you are about to dispossess, give heed to soothsayers and to diviners; but as for you, the Lord your God has not allowed you so to do."[4]

In his book *Occult Bondage and Deliverance*,[5] Dr. Kurt E. Koch says, "For years I have witnessed the truth of this fact, that magic and almost all other occult practices either destroy the Christian faith of a person or just prevent it from developing. And yet one finds that there is no conflict between sorcery and all the other world religions." This is a particularly interesting point. It is only when these evil powers come face to face with God's truth in the person of Jesus Christ that there is a serious conflict.

In God's eyes, therefore, all forms of spiritism and occultism are wrong. "When they say to you 'Consult the mediums and the wizards who chirp and mutter', should not a people consult their God? Should they consult the dead on behalf of the living? To the teaching and the testimony! [i.e. the Scriptures]. Surely for this word which they [the mediums] speak there is no dawn."[6] Certainly there is "no dawn" from spiritism: no light at all about life after death. However, in this context, with the darkness that we still have in the face of death, and with the meaninglessness and hopelessness of so much of life, we have this glorious prophecy in the very next few verses: "The people who walked in darkness have seen a great light; those who dwelt in a land of deep darkness, on them has light shined. . . . For to us a child is born, to us a son is given; and the government will be upon his shoulder, and his name will be called 'Wonderful Counsellor, Mighty God, Everlasting Father, Prince of Peace.' "[7]

Why go after dark and dangerous spirits when you can find in Jesus a Wonderful Counsellor? Why pursue unknown forces when you can find in Jesus the Mighty God, and know him as your everlasting Father? Why get involved with things that may deeply disturb you when in Jesus you can know the Prince of Peace?

Moreover, these questions are not just for those involved in spiritism. The Bible makes it clear that the whole world naturally is in the hands of the evil one, the Devil. Jesus once said to some very religious and respectable people, "You are of your father the Devil!"[8] They were shocked! However, he said that, not because they were very evil (by most external standards they were extremely good); but because they could not yet call God their Father. You can call God "Father", only when you have received Jesus into your life. "To all who received him, who believed in his name, he gave power to become children of God."[9] That is why Jesus kept on calling people out of Satan's kingdom into God's kingdom, out of Satan's family into God's family. Only in God's family can you find light and love and forgiveness and peace in any real and lasting sense.

What really happens at death? Is there any answer when there are no satisfactory answers at all from atheism, mysticism, universalism, reincarnation or spiritism? You can understand why those first Christians leapt to their feet and shouted from the housetops the most wonderful and glorious news that Jesus had been raised from the dead. Not only was he alive and with them all; but now they realized that through his death and resurrection he had destroyed death! They were absolutely convinced about it. They were willing to suffer and die for what they knew was true. Why were they so sure? Why are millions of Christians so sure today? What is the evidence that has made countless millions of people over 2,000 years convinced that Jesus rose from the dead and is alive for ever?

Other books have set forth the evidence in much greater detail,[10] but briefly it is worth considering the following points:

First, we have *the birth and growth of the Christian Church*. The disciples of Jesus were utterly despondent after the crucifixion of Christ. They had no understanding at all, in spite of repeated teaching, that Jesus would be raised from the dead. There was not a glimmer of hope. To them, after that appalling Friday, he was finished and gone. They would never see him again. When the first reports came on the Sunday that the tomb was empty and that Jesus had been seen alive, the apostles dismissed this as an old wives' tale. It was idle talk. Nothing would shake their gloom and sorrow. Now, in that context, it is historically and psychologically impossible that those disciples could suddenly have been filled with such conviction and joy that Jesus had indeed been raised from the dead, that they turned their world upside down, as their enemies had to confess. At least this is impossible unless Jesus was raised.

Second, *the New Testament could never have been written without the resurrection of Christ.* Throughout its pages there is the total assurance that Jesus was and is alive. The books of the New Testament were written at least 20 years after the death of Christ, following periods of considerable persecution, when this conviction had plenty of time to waver or die. As J. B. Phillips records, after years spent on translating these documents: "These [New Testament] letters were written over quite a period of years, but there is not the slightest discernible diminution of faith. It was borne in upon me with irresistible force that these letters could never have been written at all if there had been no Jesus Christ, no crucifixion, and no resurrection."[11]

Third, *there is the evidence of the empty tomb.* The message of the risen Christ could not have been maintained in Jerusalem for a single day if the emptiness of the tomb and the disappearance of the body had not been established as fact. No one could produce the dead body, and no one has ever put forward a satisfactory explanation for this. Clearly the *disciples* did not steal the body, for many of them died afterwards for their belief that Christ was risen. Would they have suffered martyrdom for what they knew was a lie? The *Romans* were not guilty, for they were plainly embarrassed that the body had disappeared when the tomb had been sealed and guarded by soldiers. If the *Jews* had stolen the body, they would at once have produced it to silence the preaching of the risen Christ once for all. There is only one satisfactory solution to the puzzle: Christ did indeed rise from the dead!

Fourth, *there were many resurrection appearances,* and the risen Christ was seen over a period of six weeks on eleven different occasions by a total of at least 550 people, many of whom were still alive when the evidence was recorded in the New Testament documents; and no one has ever tried to dispute this.

Fifth, *we have the testimony of millions of Christians* over 2,000 years who have known that Jesus is real and alive in their own experience. Some of these have come from other faiths; some from atheism and humanism; some from a purely nominal Christian faith. There are many today who are willing to die for what they know to be true concerning the living Christ, and it is sobering to realize that there have probably been more Christian martyrs during this century than during the rest of the history of the Christian church put together.

The Consequences
In the light of the resurrection of Christ, there are a number of important consequences.

In the first place, *the death of Christ was not a tragedy but a triumph.* All the disciples were filled with gloom at the time of the crucifixion. To them Christ's sufferings and death seemed a senseless end to a glorious life. What a tragedy! Why had God allowed it? That question was answered after the resurrection. God in Christ had dealt with the problem of sin once for all. The penalty had been paid. When Jesus cried out "It is finished!", it was not a cry of total despair, as the disciples had first thought. It was a triumphant shout: "Finished! Accomplished!" The single Greek word was sometimes stamped across bills that had been paid. *Paid*! That is what Jesus accomplished through his death. "There is no condemnation now for those who live in union with Christ Jesus."[12] And he rose again to show us that this is true.

In the second place, *the victory of Christ over Satan and all the powers of evil is complete*. Paul once wrote that, because of the death of Christ on the cross, God has "disarmed the principalities and powers".[13] He has not yet annihilated them. They are still active; they can and do cause much trouble. But like a retreating army, their power against Jesus Christ and his followers is limited.

On one university mission a young man asked if he could see me, and we planned to meet the next day. Unexpectedly he brought a girl with him. As she entered the room I had an overpowering sense of evil which filled me with sudden fear. I quietly claimed the authority and victory of Jesus over this, and the fear vanished as quickly as it had come. Then we talked; and I learned that the girl was a practicing medium, steeped in occult practices. I had no previous knowledge of this—just this sudden, powerful sense of evil. But I had also experienced the greater power of Christ! Through the death and resurrection of Christ, a Christian has nothing whatever to fear when faced with evil forces, providing he is trusting in and claiming Christ's authority and protection.

In the third place, *because of the resurrection we know that there is a life after death.* Although we cannot know the precise details, since they are outside our present total experience, we do know that this life will be unimaginably wonderful for those who love Christ. A true Christian, filled with the Spirit, will at times know something of the indescribable joy of being totally caught up in the presence of Christ. But the consummation of our relationship with Christ will be so glorious, and so beyond our present experience, that the Bible often describes it in negatives. In heaven there will be no sin, no evil, no fears, no decay, no pollution, no suffering, no loneliness, no hunger, no thirst, no sorrow: "God will wipe away every tear from their eyes."[14]

Thus, for the Christian there is nothing whatever to fear in the face of death. "I am the resurrection and the life," said Jesus. "Whoever believes in me will live, even though he dies."[15] And he rose again to show that he had the right to make such a devastating claim.

In the fourth place, however, *Christ's resurrection demonstrates the truth about judgement.* Jesus is Lord; and one day, at the name of Jesus every knee shall bow and every tongue shall confess that Jesus Christ is Lord.[16] And, unless we bow to him now as our Lord and Savior we shall *have* to bow to him one day as our Lord and Judge.

There is a legend about a man caught in a quicksand. It is no doubt a caricature, but most caricatures contain some element of the truth. Here was this man struggling and passing rapidly to his death. Confucius saw him and remarked, "There is evidence that men should stay out of such places." Buddha came and said, "Let that life be a lesson to the rest of the world." Mohammed commented, "Alas! it is the will of Allah!" A Hindu said, "Never mind, he will return to earth in another form." But when Jesus saw him he said, "Give me your hand, brother, and I will pull you out."

We are all caught in the quicksand of death. We cannot escape it. Neither Confucius, Buddha, Mohammed nor anyone else can help us or save us. At best we have only their teachings and writings. Only Jesus is alive. Therefore, only Jesus can stretch out a hand and take you into the presence of the living God forever. No wonder Paul, having considered carefully the truth of the resurrection of Christ, once cried out, "Thanks be to God who gives us the victory through our Lord Jesus Christ!"[17]

[1]*In God's Underground* by Richard Wurmbrand (Diane Books)
[2]*After Death* by Alec Motyer (Hodder & Stoughton), page 30
[3]Hebrews 9:27
[4]Deuteronomy 18:10-14
[5]Dregel
[6]Isaiah 8:19-20
[7]Isaiah 9:2, 6
[8]John 8:44
[9]John 1:12
[10]*The Evidence for the Resurrection* by Prof. J. N. D. Anderson (Inter-Varsity), *Christianity The Witness of History* by Prof. J. N. D. Anderson (IVP), *Man Alive* by Michael Green (IVP), *Who Moved the Stone* by Frank Morison (Zondervan).
[11]*Ring of Truth* (Macmillan)
[12]Romans 8:1 (TEV)
[13]Colossians 2:15
[14]Revelation 7:15-17, See also Revelation 21-22
[15]John 11:25 (TEV)
[16]Philippians 2:10f
[17]1 Corinthians 15:57

7
OPEN
TO
LIFE

The morning service had just finished in Washington Cathedral, and the congregation was streaming out to greet their English guest preacher, who happened to be me. "Could I see you sometime?" asked a young man, who had obviously been stirred by something in the sermon.

Later that day Richard and I were deep in conversation. Richard was obviously gifted and intelligent, the son of a judge, and himself a law student at the University of Virginia. He was at that time holding a vacation job—a cab driver in the city of Washington, D.C.

At the end of a long but extremely valuable conversation, when I sensed that the Spirit of God was working quietly but deeply in Richard's life, we knelt and prayed. Very simply Richard asked Jesus Christ to become his Lord and Savior and to enter his life by his Holy Spirit.

Before we parted I explained that though there might be no sudden or dramatic experience, increasingly he would know the reality of Christ as he sought to deepen this new-found relationship. I gave him a little guidance about this. I had no further contact or correspondence with Richard until he wrote to me three months later.

"It took me a few weeks to realize it but the fact is that something has been very different about my whole life since my conversion; I still can't describe exactly what the difference is. There is a tremendous sense of a load off my shoulders, of an end of running around 'like a chicken with his head chopped off,' of relief in general, of joy, peace and happiness, but those words only begin to do the job. There is an absolute certainty of the presence in my life of an Individual who cares about me more than I could ever care about anyone else; who knows and shares my every thought, joy or care; of whom I can ask anything; and who is always, always there. It is too good to be true, or so it would seem, and yet it is as real as night and day."

Richard, of course, is only one of hundreds of thousands who can speak of the same transformation in their lives. They may be of different ages, from different backgrounds, education, culture, race and color, and yet there is one obvious common factor. They all speak of a new life in Jesus Christ. I am not saying that they never have any doubts or problems, but increasingly they know that something radical has happened which concerns the whole of their lives. It is the Spirit of God who has come to live in them as they put their trust in Christ. Without this fact, there would be no Christian Church at all. Indeed, the whole spiritual revolution that Christ inaugurated would have died a natural death in the first century.

During the earthly ministry of Jesus, his disciples were wholly dependent on him. Without him they were often faithless, fearful and foolish. Frequently Jesus had to say to them, "O you of little faith!" "Have you no faith?" "Why did you doubt?" Often they missed the point altogether. Sometimes they failed miserably. And at the time of supreme testing, with the events leading up to the crucifixion, one betrayed Jesus, another denied him, and all deserted him when the going proved too tough. This was not very promising material for the start of the greatest revolution the world has ever seen. Moreover, just before Christ's ascension into heaven, his disciples asked him when he would finish the job for them. When would he throw out the Roman occupation and restore the kingdom to Israel? This is how he replied: "You will be filled with power when the Holy Spirit comes on you; and you will be witnesses for me in Jerusalem, in all of Judea and Samaria, and to the ends of the earth."[1] A moment later he left them—for good.

Of course, they felt helpless and very frightened. They huddled behind locked doors, afraid of the Jews. They had no power and no wish to witness to Jesus, especially in Jerusalem where their Master had been so recently murdered. All they could possibly do was to hold on to this promise of the Spirit of God. And it is a historical fact that something very remarkable happened. These ordinary, timid disciples were filled with a new life and a new confidence that they had never known before. They were possessed with a love and a joy and a power which gave them immense boldness and authority wherever they went. Many thousands found the living Christ; the sick were healed; signs and wonders took place in the name of Jesus. They were opposed, beaten, imprisoned, killed. But on and on they went. As J. B. Phillips expressed it in his preface to the Acts of the Apostles, "It is a matter of sober historical fact that never before has any small body of ordinary people so moved the world that their enemies could say with tears of rage in their eyes that these men have turned the world upside down!"

What had brought about this change? There was no dynamic leader, no successor to Jesus Christ. It was the promised Holy Spirit, come to dwell in the life of every true believer in Christ. Paul once wrote, "When someone becomes a Christian he becomes a brand new person inside. He is not the same any more. A new life has begun!"[2]

How else can you explain historical facts like these? What other explanation can there be for the birth and beginnings? What of the testimonies of millions of people right up to the present day who speak of this new life? It is true that the record of the Church, as an *institution,* has been very mixed. No one can defend, on Christian terms, the religious wars or persecutions, the pseudo-religious conflict in Northern Ireland, or the hypocrises and inconsistencies of the Church which drove Karl Marx to Communism and Sigmund Freud to psychoanalysis. It is all too obvious why some have been driven away from a vital faith in Christ because of the obstacle of the Church.

However, it is important to remember two truths. First, *religion* and *true Christianity* can be two very different things. It was religious people who most of all opposed Christ and finally crucified him. And religion has frequently been the enemy of the real thing—the Devil's counterfeit. Second, even within the true Christian church, Christ said there would always be both *wheat* and *tares*, both the good and the bad, which would not be separated until the final day of judgement. One good definition of the Church is that it is "Christ's hospital". If I visit a hospital which claims to heal sick people, and find it full of sick people, I do not say "What a wretched hospital! What hypocrisy!" Instead, I am glad to know that it is in touch with the right people. Likewise the Church is a fellowship of sinners. If its members are still morally and spiritually imperfect in various degrees, it is not a denial of the truth of the Christian faith, but only that the Church is in touch with the right people. It is part of the evidence of the Holy Spirit that he can take such very ordinary, selfish, sinful human beings, and do as much *in* them and *through* them as he has done all down the centuries. It is part of the reality of the Spirit that the Church, in spite of all its numerous faults and failings, still exists, and in some parts of the world is expanding more rapidly than the exploding birth rate itself.

Let us look further at this new life brought to us by the Holy Spirit as we put our trust in Jesus Christ; drawing our thoughts mainly from one of the great chapters in the Bible on the Spirit's work, Romans 8.

The Spirit sets us free from the self-life

"For the law of the Spirit of life in Christ Jesus has set me free from the law of sin and death."[3] In the first seven chapters of Romans, Paul has been expounding on man's situation in the sight of God. Everyone can know something about God: his reality and power have been clearly revealed in the things that have been made. We see the evidence of God in the design and wonder of creation all around us. Further, God's laws and moral standards are also known, to some extent at least, by our conscience even if we are totally ignorant of God's self-revelation in the Bible and in his Son Jesus Christ. However, the truth is this: whatever knowledge of God's laws we may or may not have had, we have all fallen far short of his perfect standards, or even of our own imperfect standards. Therefore we have all sinned in God's eyes and desperately need to be forgiven and to be made right with God. In Romans 5 Paul uses four words to describe our situation. We are *helpless* and cannot live as God wants us to live; we are *ungodly* and do not put God at the centre of our lives where he ought to be; we are *sinners* because we break God's commandments; we are *enemies* and go our own way, not God's way doing what we want, not what God wants. Next to those four words Paul puts one fact:

> While we were yet helpless . . . *Christ died*
> *Christ died* for the ungodly
> While we were yet sinners *Christ died*
> While we were enemies we were reconciled to God by the *death of his Son.*

Four times, therefore, Paul presents the cross of Christ as the answer to man's supreme problem, sin. Elsewhere in the New Testament the truth shines out as clearly as can be. "Now in Christ Jesus you who were once far off have been brought near in the blood of Christ."[4] "We have confidence to enter the sanctuary [i.e. God's presence] by the blood of Jesus."[5] "Christ also died for sins once for all, the righteous for the unrighteous, that he might bring us to God."[6] No one can find God or come to God except through the blood of God's own Son Jesus Christ. This is our only hope of reconciliation. But having come to God through Jesus we still need something more.

The humanist Walter Lippman made this perceptive comment after the last World War, "We ourselves were so sure that at long last a generation had arisen, keen and eager to put this disorderly earth to right . . . and fit to do it. . . . We meant so well, we tried so hard, and look what we have made of it. We can only muddle into muddle. What is required is a new kind of man."

It is because of this that God offers us not only a Savior to take away the guilt of the past, but also his Spirit to transform our lives here and now. You see, the things that spoil our lives most of all—and the lives of others too—are not the things around us but the things within us. It is from within, out of the very heart of man, that all the problems spring.[7] These are the things that pull me down; my selfishness, my greed, my self-pity, my resentment. And the trouble is that, when I try to overcome these problems myself, I find that I simply cannot do it. Paul expresses this frustration in vivid terms: "For I know that nothing good dwells within me, that is, in my flesh. I can will what is right, but I cannot do it. For I do not do the good I want, but the evil I do not want is what I do. . . . Wretched man that I am! Who will deliver me from this body of death?"[8] Then after this cry of despair we find a sudden burst of praise and release in the next breath: "For the law of the Spirit of life in Christ Jesus has set me free from the law of sin and death."[9]

How can Paul swing so suddenly from one experience to the other? The key to it all is this: in the depressing last ten verses of Romans 7 Paul mentions "I" 25 times and "me" or "my" 13 times. Here we have 38 references to himself in ten verses! And the Holy Spirit is not mentioned once. But in Romans 8 the Holy Spirit is mentioned 19 times with "I" only twice. It is the Holy Spirit who sets us free from all that spoils our lives. Naturally the law of sin and death brings us down; but the Spirit of life in Christ Jesus not only overcomes the downward pull of sin and death but lifts us up into a new quality of life altogether. It is the self-life that is responsible for all those attitudes and actions that cause such misery: "immorality, impurity, licentiousness, idolatry, sorcery, enmity, strife, jealousy, anger, selfishness, dissension, party spirit, envy, drunkenness, carousing, and the like."[10] However, the Spirit's life is gloriously different: "Love, joy, peace, patience, kindness, goodness, faithfulness, gentleness, self-control."[11] And that transformation is not only a fact in human experience, but it is perhaps the greatest miracle that we could ever witness. The Jewish philosopher, Martin Buber, once asked, "Is there any force in the world that can change that intractable thing, human nature? There's a tragedy at the heart of things." There is no force in the world that can change the heart of man; it is only the Spirit of Jesus who can make us into his likeness. One woman changed so much when she met with Christ that she thought it best to send a new photograph to be attached to her passport. But even she was surprised when an official from the passport office rang to say that it was impossible to stick the new photo beside the old one because it looked like an entirely different person. He told her that she must now apply for a new passport, with signatures to confirm that it really was the same person![12]

No one is claiming for a moment that a Christian is perfect. In fact, it is perhaps only the Christian who realizes just how imperfect he really is. All the great men and women of God have been deeply conscious of their own faults and failings, and have longed to be more like Jesus. John Newton once summed it up neatly like this: "I am not what I ought to be; I am not what I would like to be; I am not yet what I hope to be. But I am not what I was; and by the grace of God I am what I am."

Moreover when a person is increasingly full of an unusually rich quality of love, joy and peace, then that person knows something of real wealth. The whole world is often going crazy in search of these things, but they come to us in the fullest and richest sense when the Spirit of God comes to dwell within us. As one woman wrote to me, "I have had many joys in my life, but the most wonderful joy of them all is the rebirth in Jesus Christ. It's made a tremendous difference; the love of Jesus is always there—new and fresh every morning."

The Spirit sets us free to enjoy God
In Paul's words, "The old sinful nature within us is against God. . . . It can never please God. But you are not like that. You are controlled by your new nature if you have the Spirit of God living in you."[13]

I have always loved the question asked in the Scottish Catechism: "What is the chief end of man?" It is the question that people are asking all over the world at this moment. The answer is: "To glorify God and to enjoy him forever." How far do you *enjoy* God? Is he a real person in your life? Does he fill you with such a quality of life and joy that you could never find anywhere else? The purpose of life is not to have an academic discussion about the possibility of God's existence. It is to enjoy him, to know him, to love him and to experience his love in our own lives. That is the chief end of man! Jesus said exactly the same thing: eternal life, the life for which God created and made us, is summed up in knowing God and knowing Jesus Christ.[14] We have not opened up to life until we have opened up to God. It is something so significantly and fundamentally new that Jesus called it a new birth, a spiritual birth which is essential before we can come to know God, since God is Spirit.

When a thoroughly respectable and religious man came to Jesus one night because he was interested in this unusual preacher, Jesus said to him, in effect, three things: "You must be born again! You must be born again! You must be born again!" He said it three times for emphasis. Why? Because unless a man is born again he cannot see the Kingdom of God—he is blind to it— and he cannot live in the Kingdom of God —he is dead to it. Therefore, it is imperative that each person must be born again before he can come into God's presence and kingdom.[15] A Rector of a large and prosperous church, the Reverend Charles Jarman who held several university degrees in theology, said this: "I preached for 52 years before I knew the Lord Jesus as my personal Savior! True, I was a minister, and thought I was a Christian, but that did not make me one." And in the story of his life he recorded how on March 28th, 1966, he knelt down and for the first time asked Christ to come into his life. "I have never felt such peace. . . . I knew that I was born again in Christ Jesus."

It does not matter who a person is, a bishop, minister, theologian, respectable agnostic, militant atheist, or faithful churchgoer. Unless that person is born again by the Spirit of God he can neither see nor enter the Kingdom of God. So says the Son of God! Of course it is tragic if a person shows no interest in this new birth. God longs that each of us should enjoy him—not discuss him, nor debate him, nor argue about him but simply enjoy him. There are countless Christians all over the world whose lives could speak eloquently of the joy that Jesus brings. One student told me, with her eyes sparkling with life, of the "incredible joy of the Holy Spirit, a joy bubbling up inside" her.

The Spirit sets us free to pray to God

"Those who are led by God's Spirit are God's sons. For the Spirit that God has given you does not make you a slave and cause you to be afraid; instead, the Spirit makes you God's sons, and by the Spirit's power we cry to God, 'Father! my Father!' "[16]

The Spirit, therefore, helps us to enjoy God, not only in terms of the highs when there is a great time of worship and praise with other Christians, or when we may have special spiritual experiences, but in developing our whole relationship with God so that something deep down within us wants to cry out "Abba! Father!"

Often there are two fears about a personal commitment to Christ. First there is a fear that there may be a very sudden change so that we are perfectly normal one day and super-religious the next! The truth is, of course, that it very seldom happens like that. Although there is a new birth which is both decisive and wonderful, it is a new birth leading to a new relationship; and very few relationships explode overnight. Normally they develop gradually. Certainly there may be some things which need to be put right at once; but other changes will occur slowly but surely as the friendship with Jesus becomes more real and personal. This may have the effect of making some other pursuits in life hollow and superficial in comparison.

The second fear is, "I could never keep it up." The answer is that in our own strength we are right. But the Spirit of God comes to live within us, helping us to do the very things that we could not do ourselves. Paul says, "The Spirit helps us in our weakness." In particular he helps us to develop our relationship with God. He helps us to understand the Bible, so that we begin to see how God can speak to us day by day. He helps us to pray, so that quite naturally we begin to talk to God and share our life with him and let him share his life with us. The Spirit helps us to overcome some of the sins in our lives, changing our selfishness into love, our pride into humility, our greed into generosity. The Spirit helps us to know God, to live for God, to bring the reality of God to other people, to love other people. There is not an area in our life that the Holy Spirit cannot enrich with his presence and power. Certainly Jesus wants to be Lord of our lives, otherwise he cannot transform our lives according to his best plan for us. But in every way he helps us to fulfil that plan by his Spirit. As a seed planted in the ground grows up into something beautiful and fragrant, so the Holy Spirit within us, planted in our hearts when we respond personally to Jesus, begins a process which develops into a beautiful personal relationship with the living God.

The Spirit sets us free from all fear

Fear can be an extraordinarily powerful factor in our lives. We may be afraid of other people, afraid of what they may think or say about us. Perhaps we are afraid of our future, or of pain, sickness or death. Well, the promise of Paul is clear: "For we know that in all things God works for good with those who love him, those whom he has called according to his purpose.... If God is for us who can be against us? He did not even keep back his own Son, but offered him for us all! He gave us his Son—will he not also freely give us all things?... For I am certain that nothing can separate us from his love: neither death nor life; neither angels nor other heavenly rulers or powers; neither the present nor the future, neither the world above nor the world below—there is nothing in all creation that will ever be able to separate us from the love of God which is ours through Christ Jesus our Lord."[17]

One summer I met a lovely girl who had a little baby. Her husband was in the Army and on a particularly dangerous mission in Vietnam. She told me how she had been full of fear, for him, for her baby, and for herself. Then God gave her the faith to believe these promises from Romans 8, and it was perfectly obvious to me that she was filled with God's peace.

The Christian knows, through the death and resurrection of Jesus, that even when death does come we are not separated from God's love. We are simply more fully and perfectly in God's presence than ever before.

[1]Acts 1:8 (TEV)
[2]II Corinthians 5:17 (*Living Bible*)
[3]Romans 8:2
[4]Ephesians 2:13
[5]Hebrews 10:19
[6]1 Peter 3:18
[7]Mark 7:21-23
[8]Romans 7:18, 19, 24
[9]Romans 8:2
[10]Galatians 5:19-21
[11]Galatians 5:22f
[12]Told by Basilea Schlink in *You Will Never Be The Same* (Bethany Fellowship).
[13]Romans 8:7-9 (*Living Bible*)
[14]John 17:3
[15]See John 3:1-7
[16]Romans 8:14-16
[17]Romans 8:28, 31-32, 38-39 (TEV)

8
WHY
BOTHER?

Apathy rules the day! "Yes, I am interested in the Christian faith. Perhaps there is a God. Maybe Jesus is alive. I'll think about it—sometime." The majority of people today are neither for Christ nor against Christ. They may be interested; they may be impressed; they may be in search of God; but they do not want to get personally involved with Christ and with the Christian faith.

In this chapter, let us focus attention on one man who had to make up his mind about Jesus: Pontius Pilate, Roman governor of Judea. He tried very hard to remain neutral, and did not want to be personally involved with the intriguing yet puzzling figure of Jesus. He was frankly disturbed when Jesus was brought as a prisoner before him; and, although he struggled first of all with the crowd and then with his own conscience, he tried to wash his hands of the whole business. "When Pilate saw that he was gaining nothing, but rather that a riot was beginning, he took water and washed his hands before the crowd, saying 'I am innocent of this man's blood: see to it yourselves.' "[1]

However, concerning the great issues of life and death, God and man, there is no neutral position at all. These are issues which inevitably affect every single one of us. We cannot remain uninvolved. Christ spoke with immense authority about the meaning and purpose of life, about death and what happens after death, about the nature of man and the nature of God, about the need of man in the sight of God, about sin, forgiveness, love and peace. And concerning these issues, with many others like them, there can be no neutral position because these are part of our very life and death. We may refuse to make up our minds on these matters but we cannot refuse to make up our life. Our life is being made up in one direction or other all the time.

The Nationalist Chinese Foreign Minister at the United Nations General Assembly in 1961 quoted the following definition from the Peking New Terminology Dictionary: "*Neutralist line*: a daydream that can never be realized. Even its theory is not correct. There are only two roads, either to support capitalism or to support socialism. There is no third road. Any vain hope to take on a third road is doomed to failure." A Christian dictionary might give a very similar definition: "*Neutralist line*: a daydream that can never be realized. Even its theory is not correct. There are only two roads, one leading to life and the other leading to destruction. There is no third road. Any vain hope to take on a third road is doomed to failure."

Why then do people doubt? Why are so few willing to get personally involved with Christ? Let us look more carefully at Pontius Pilate. Basically, there were two reasons why he tried so hard to remain neutral.

He was not sure about Christ

At least he was not 100% sure. There were some questions he just could not answer. The more he studied Christ, the more he was puzzled and mystified. "Now Jesus stood before the governor; and the governor asked him, 'Are you the King of the Jews?' Jesus said to him, 'You have said so.' But when he was accused by the chief priests and elders,, he made no answer. Then Pilate said to him, 'Do you not hear how many things they testify against you?' But he gave him no answer not even to a single charge; so that the governor wondered greatly."[2]

Many today also are confused and unsure about Christ. And they want to be completely and absolutely sure before they are prepared to act. Nevertheless, in my experience, there are many reasons for doubt. Let me give some of them.

Prejudice. A student once said, "I've made up my mind; don't confuse me with facts!" Most of us are creatures of prejudice to some extent. I can understand a person who has been disillusioned by what may seem to be stuffy, established, church-ianity. The vital thing, however, is to be open and honest, and willing to change your mind. There is nothing so deadly as a closed mind.

There was a man who once thought that he was dead. Nothing that his parents, doctors, friends or psychiatrists could do could persuade him otherwise. One psychiatrist, however, worked out a plan of action. After studying together a medical textbook, he managed to convince the man of one simple fact: dead men do not bleed. "Yes, I agree," said the man, "dead men do not bleed!" Whereupon the psychiatrist plunged a small knife into the man's arm and the blood started to flow. The man looked at his arm, his face white with astonishment and horror. "Goodness me!" he said. "Dead men do bleed after all!"

Now in one sense that man was already dead, because he was not alive to reality; he was unable to change his mind. And many today are spiritually dead in that they will not consider the possibility that Christ might be right and they might be wrong. Prejudice is a most destructive and dangerous thing.

Insufficient evidence. I was having breakfast in an Oxford college a few years ago, with an intelligent lawyer sitting opposite me. Having discovered I was a clergyman he said, "I'm an atheist. What are you going to do with me?" I replied, "As a lawyer you will appreciate the need to consider the evidence carefully before coming to any verdict. Have you considered the evidence for Jesus Christ?" It was soon transparently clear that he was very largely ignorant of the evidence for Christ, and had more or less dismissed the Christian faith on quite superficial grounds. He knew almost nothing about the historical reliability of the New Testament documents, the solid substantial evidence of the person of Christ or the resurrection of Christ, the facts relating to the formation of the Christian Church, and the personal experience of countless millions of Christians down the centuries.

This is tragic. Jesus said that our response to him was of vital importance, affecting both our life and the whole of eternity. The meaning of our present existence depends on our relationship with him. What happens at death depends upon our response to him. Questions of forgiveness, peace and hope are all wrapped up in him. The person and teaching of Jesus must radically affect every single one of us. At least we ought to examine the evidence as carefully as possible. And if we do that, it is certainly powerful enough to lead us to take a rational step of faith.

No sense of need. "I am perfectly all right as I am; I don't need a god crutch." The real question, of course, is not "Do I feel a need?" but "Is it true?" In the physical realm it is possible to suffer from euphoria: you may feel astonishingly well while in fact you are sick. There is also a spiritual euphoria. This is what Jesus made so clear. And the one person with the qualifications to speak about our need before God kept on saying that, whether we feel it or not, we have a tremendous need, so great that he was willing to die for us on the cross to make it possible for us to be forgiven.

For example, look at the commandments of God. It is not what I think about God that matters; it is what God thinks about me that really counts. And he has given us very clear instructions and commandments. Let me put the Ten Commandments in the form of questions. Have you always put God first in your life where he ought to be? Have you never put anything in the place of God in your life? Have you never taken his name, or the name of Jesus carelessly on your lips? Have you always kept one day a week for worship and rest? Have you always respected and honored your parents? Have you never hated anyone, never become bitter, resentful? Have you never had sex outside marriage, never harbored impure thoughts or lusts and desires? Have you never stolen, not even a person's reputation? Have you never told a lie or half-truth about another person? Have you never coveted what is not yours? Covetousness is perhaps the major sin of today. If you have ever failed in any of those points, then you are guilty before God, under his judgement, and in desperate need of his forgiveness. If that were not true, said Paul, Christ died for nothing!

Therefore it is not a question of feeling a need, but of being humble enough to listen to Christ, to hear what he says and see what he did, supremely on the cross. "I am the way . . . no one comes to the Father but by me." A person is free to ignore him if he wants to; but he is not free to ignore the consequences.

Once bitten, twice shy.   "I've tried before, but it hasn't worked." If that is so I can understand a person's hesitation, but let me say three things about this. In the first place, did you really begin a personal *relationship* with Jesus? I was confirmed 11 years before taking that step. I had tried, I had turned over a new leaf; but how different it was when I found a new life.!

Then, did you go on to *deepen* that relationship with Jesus? All relationships must be developed. Most relationships do not blossom overnight, and they need to be worked at. As soon as we take any relationship for granted, that is the beginning of trouble.

Third, do not try to analyse too precisely what may have happened in the past. Perhaps you have already committed your life "in pencil" years ago. Well now, ink it over. God wants you to be quite sure about your relationship with him.

Fear. A brilliant young lawyer openly admitted what was holding him back from a personal commitment to Christ, saying, "It is the fear of getting involved." Many people know this: a fear that Christ may upset their social life, their ambitions, or their plans. A fear of losing a few friends, a fear of what their friends might say, a fear of being laughed at.

Fortunately Jesus was not afraid of those things. For our sake, to take away the guilt of our sin, he was willing to be "despised and rejected by men, a man of sorrows and acquainted with grief". He was willing to be "wounded for our transfressions, bruised for our iniquities". He was willing to be "oppressed, stricken, afflicted". He became the sacrificial offering for our sins as the Lord laid on him the guilt of us all.[3] If ever we are afraid of getting involved, we need to look carefully at the cross of Jesus Christ. Our fears, frankly, are a pathetic mixture of pride, self-centredness, and short-sightedness. Jesus, in his love, gave us many, many warnings of the judgement to come if we try to remain neutral. "What does it profit a man to gain the whole world and forfeit his life?"[4] "On that day many will say to me 'Lord, Lord did we not . . . do many mighty works in your name?' and then will I declare to them, 'I never knew you; depart from me. . . .' "[5] So much of his teaching contains realistic warnings as to what will happen if we choose to ignore or reject him. He is willing, in his love, to warn us of the folly of neglect because he longs that we might know his love and friendship in our own experience.

Returning to Pontius Pilate, I do not think he was really so unsure about Christ. He knew perfectly well, for example, that Christ was innocent. There was almost certainly another reason which made Pilate determined to remain neutral if at all possible.

He was not willing to get involved
There were probably two reasons at least for this.

In the first place he was influenced by the crowd. On that first Good Friday, being the time of the feast of the Passover, it was the custom of the governor to release one prisoner. One half of him wanted very much to release Jesus. "He asked them, 'Do you want me to release for you the King of the Jews?' For he perceived that it was out of envy that the chief priests had delivered him up. But the chief priests stirred up the crowd to have him release for them Barabbas instead. And Pilate again said to them, 'Then what shall I do with the man whom you call the King of the Jews?' And they cried out again, 'Crucify him.' And Pilate said to them, 'Why, what evil has he done?' But they shouted all the more, 'Crucify him.' So Pilate, wishing to satisfy the crowd, released for them Barabbas; and having sourged Jesus, he delivered him to be crucified."[6]

There we have it: *wishing to satisfy the crowd*. Many have the same pull in their lives. What we may not realize is that some of our "crowd", however self-confident or rebellious they may appear on the surface, are probably deep-down hungry for God or for some kind of spiritual reality themselves. How foolish if we hold back because of our friends!

Then there was his personal ambition. The Jewish

ringleaders threw down their trump card! "If you release this man, you are not Caesar's friend!" That did it! At once Jesus was sent to the cross.

The question is, How successfully did Pilate remain neutral and uninvolved? In one sense the answer is obvious. For 2,000 years millions of Christians have said each week in the Apostles' Creed, "Jesus Christ crucified under Pontius Pilate." There is no neutral position.

More than that, Pilate suffered later from a bad conscience. According to Greek historians, shortly after this incident he committed suicide in Rome. No doubt there were other reasons as well, but no one can finally silence his conscience.

Poor Pilate missed the whole truth about life, even though it was there right in front of him. "What is truth?" he asked rhetorically. And there was Jesus standing before him, the man who had said "I am the truth." But Pilate missed it.

One further step

So far in our search for God we have looked at some of the evidence for God's self-revelation in his Son. We have looked at Jesus yesterday, seeing something of the historical facts of his person, his death and his resurrection, and the development of the Christian church. We have looked at Jesus today, seeing his reality in the lives of many different people from many different backgrounds. However, there is still one final piece of evidence that anyone can have, and indeed must have, when they have done all the reading, talking and thinking in the world. You can discover the reality of God when you come to know Jesus for yourself, when you sincerely ask him to come into your life. Nothing that I could say, or anyone else could say, can substitute for that.

One young person at a special service asked Christ to come into her life. Six weeks later she wrote to me to say how very real it had all become in her experience. Then she said this in her letter, "I'd been thinking carefully, but warily, about Christianity for a long time. . . . That evening was a great step forward because for the first time I felt truly involved in the whole experience of finding Christ. Previously I had argued intellectually from a distance, but although I was becoming more and more convinced that Jesus had all the answers, I still did not feel near to the heart of it all. . . . Now I realize that no matter how much arguing is done about the historical evidence for Jesus, etc., *the only answer is to enter into a personal relationship with Jesus himself,* and then he will help you and will answer your questions." That is the heart of it all. A person may talk for 3,000 years and still go round and round in circles. "The only answer is to enter into a personal relationship with Jesus himself." This is the most important thing we can do in our life. Without this we have no God, no hope, nothing of ultimate value.

How, then, can we become personally involved?

---

[1]Matthew 27:24
[2]Matthew 27:11-14
[3]See Isaiah 53
[4]Mark 8:36
[5]Matthew 7:22f
[6]Mark 15:9-15

9

FINDING GOD

To one genuine seeker Jesus said, "Zacchaeus, hurry up and come down. I must be your guest today!"[1] So Zacchaeus, who (from a mixture of fascination and fear) was hiding in a sycamore tree, "hurriedly climbed down and gladly welcomed him".

How many of us are like Zacchaeus! One half of us wants to know the truth about God and longs for Jesus to become real and personal in our lives. We see the evidence and we talk with friends who have found him. And yet we are afraid. What will others say? What will Jesus do? How much will my life have to change? Am I losing my independence? There's too much to give up! Most of us know this tug-of-war inside us.

Jesus today
One thing is clear. When Jesus calls us by name (and in our heart or conscience we seem to know deep down when that is so) there is some urgency about it. "Hurry up!" he says. "I must be your guest *today*!" Jesus is *today's* man. God's time is always today, and the Scrip-

tures frequently make this clear: "Today, when you hear his voice, do not harden your hearts";[2] "Now is the acceptable time . . . now is the day of salvation";[3] "Seek the Lord while he may be found, call upon him while he is near."[4]

How then can we welcome Jesus into the house of our life? Four words may clarify the steps that we need to take: Turn, Trust, Take and Thank.

Turn. If I realize that I have been going my own way through life, I must be willing to turn right round and go with Jesus. This is what the Bible calls *repentance*. Repentance means much more than being sorry for sin. Feeling sorry can all too easily spring from self-pity. Rather, I must humbly admit that I have broken God's laws, rebelled against him, hurt him, and displeased him; and now I am willing to turn right away from all that I know is wrong in my life. If I am willing to do that, and to turn round to Jesus, taking him with both hands, then I have taken the first vital step. Zacchaeus, the well-known swindler, said to Jesus, "Look, sir, I will give half my property to the poor. And if I have swindled anybody out of anything I will pay him back four times as much."

Don't worry if you are not yet sure of all the wrong things in your life. God, in his gentleness, shows us our wrongdoings step by step. But you cannot hold on to what you *know* is wrong in one hand, and try to take Jesus with the other. It simply does not work. Jesus is not interested in compromise—any more than a dentist is happy to leave four bad teeth in your mouth just because you asked him to deal only with the one that hurts!

Trust. I must trust Jesus in two ways. First I must trust him as my *Savior*, who has taken all my sin upon himself when he died on the Cross. This is the only way I could ever come into God's presence. And, wonderfully, Christ has paid the penalty for all my sin; there is nothing for me to pay.

I must also trust Jesus as my *Lord*, inviting him into my life, not only as Guest, but as Master and Owner. Every part of my life must now come under his control: my plans and ambitions, my business life and social life, my study and sport, my home and family, girl-friend or boy-friend, husband or wife. And I must trust him as Lord of all these things because he alone always know what is best. He never comes to spoil my life—only to enrich it. He cares about my well-being more than anyone ever could. Therefore he must take control as Lord of all.

Take. "The free gift of God is eternal life in Christ Jesus our Lord."[5] Although God offers me this priceless gift—the gift of his own Son—if I do not take it, I will not have it. It is tragically as simple as that. God will not throw his gifts at me, whether I want them or not. He waits for me to stretch out my empty hands and take from him this most valuable gift that I could ever have, the gift of eternal life in Jesus Christ.

In practice how do I take it, or take *him*? Zacchaeus simply "welcomed" Jesus into his house; and Jesus said, "Salvation has come to this house today!"

A famous promise of Jesus is in Revelation 3:20: "Behold, I stand at the door and knock; if anyone hears my voice and opens the door, I will come in to him. . . ." The picture is quite clear. If you are sitting at home waiting for a friend to arrive, and suddenly you hear a knock, what do you do? Of course you get up and open the door; and if it is your friend, you say "Come in!" You have now welcomed him into your house.

So it is with Jesus. In simple words I must ask him to come into my life. And as soon as I do that and mean it, then I receive Jesus—or more accurately, I receive the Spirit of Jesus, the Holy Spirit—into my life. A new relationship with God—Father, Son and Spirit—has now begun.

Thank. The essence of all relationships is faith, and faith means taking a person at his word. No relationship would be possible if I did not believe a person's word. Again, so it is with Jesus. Whether or not I feel anything when I ask Jesus to come in, I must believe that he *has* come in, because that is his solemn word. Therefore, in faith, I say "Thank you!" As with so many aspects of life, it is only when we *act* as though something were true that it ever becomes true. For example, it is only when I take a check to my bank that it will ever become true in my account!

With Jesus, then, I must believe his promise, thank him that he is now in my life (having invited him), and begin to act as though it were true. It *is* true, and it will wonderfully become true in my experience. "Whatever you ask in prayer," said Jesus, "believe that you receive it, *and you will.*"[6]

Have you ever personally asked Jesus into your life? Are you quite sure? Are you sure that he is now with you? Is God real in your experience? If the answer to any of those questions is "No," then you could pray a prayer now, quietly and simply, wherever you are. If possible, of course, get alone somewhere, and many people find it helpful to kneel when they pray. Here are words you could use.

"Lord Jesus Christ, I admit that I have sinned and have gone my own way. I am willing to turn, with your help, from all that I know is wrong. I believe that you died for me to take away my sins; and I want you to be the Lord and Master of my life. And now I ask you to come in. Come into my life, Lord Jesus, to be my Savior, my Friend and my Lord for ever. Thank you, Lord Jesus. Amen."

Have you now prayed that? Well, believe that Jesus has *now answered your prayer* and has come into your life in the person of the Holy Spirit. As from now seek to live each day knowing that he is with you and will never leave you.

Jesus every day

That personal prayer, of course, was only a beginning: a vital, indispensable step, but much more is to follow, as in every true relationship. The Christian life is not a matter of rules and regulations, nor of feelings and experiences—primarily—but a steady, deepening relationship for the rest of one's life. When you meet someone for the first time it is unlikely that there will be a radical change in your life overnight. Normally the friendship must deepen, and that takes time.[7]

It may be helpful to think of three sets of relationships.

My relationship with God

The apostle Peter once wrote, "You have been born

anew, not of perishable seed but of imperishable, through the living and abiding word of God. . . . That word is the good news which was preached to you."[8] When you invite Christ into your life, the Holy Spirit begins within you a spiritual birth. You are therefore "born again", born into God's family. Let me answer some common question.

1. "How do I know that I am born again?"
John answers that in his first letter. It is like sitting on a three-legged stool. If all three legs are there, you are in a stable position! If only two or one support you, there may be trouble! What are these 'legs'?

First, the Word of God (1 John 5:11-12). We must trust Christ's promise,[9] being quietly confident that he really means what he says.

Second, the work of Christ (1 John 1:7). All our sins, without exception, are washed clean by the blood of Jesus. Because of this, we can have absolute assurance of our relationship with God.[10]

Third, the witness of the Spirit. John talks of many new developments in our life that can assure us of our new birth: a new desire to please God, a new love for God, a new hatred for sin, a new love for God's people, a new peace, a new power over temptation, a new reality in prayer. . . .[11] Like the blossom and fruit on a tree, these things will normally grow and develop over a period of time. Together with these, there should be a deep inward assurance that God is our Father and we his children.[12]

2. "How can I grow in this new life?"
Peter answers, "Like newborn babes, long for the pure

spiritual milk, that by it you may grow up to salvation; for you have tasted the kindness of the Lord."[13]

As with every relationship we must spend time with Christ, primarily through personal Bible reading and prayer. Through the Bible Jesus can speak to us; through prayer we speak to him. Every day, if we possibly can, we need to find time, or *make* time (it is never easy), when we can be alone and quiet in his presence. Most Christians find that first thing in the morning, before the rush of the day has started, is the best time. For others, such as young mothers, that may be almost impossible. But we need to fight for these times when our relationship with Jesus can grow. A modern translation of the Bible such as The Living Bible, Today's English Version or The New International Version is very helpful. There are various Bible reading methods,[14] and it is wise to start with one of the Gospels, perhaps Mark or John. Many of the Psalms, too, are especially helpful,[15] and some of the shorter letters of the New Testament.[16] Before you read, ask God to help you to understand the passage; the Bible is a spiritual book and we need the Holy Spirit to illuminate our minds with its truth. Moreover, we shall grasp God's truth insofar as we are willing to obey what is written.

Let God speak to you through the verses you are reading. Meditate on them or mentally "chew them over," thinking quietly both about their meaning and about their special meaning for you. What is God saying here to *you,* in your situation today? Then talk back to God in prayer, using some of the thoughts from the Bible passage as the basis for your prayers. In this way a real two-way conversation between you and God can develop. There are, of course, many aspects of prayer,[17] including:

Worship and praise, praising God for who he is and what he has done, both in creation and redemption. Many of the Psalms are helpful for this, and various New Testament passages such as Revelation 4 and 5.

Thanksgiving, thanking God for specific blessings or answers to prayer.

Confession, bringing before God anything on your conscience, being willing to turn right away from all that you know is wrong. Claim some promise of God's forgiveness such as 1 John 1:7, 9.

Intercession, praying for the needs of others and of yourself. Many find some simple prayer list or calendar of real help. You cannot pray for everyone every day! Therefore divide up the list of names and needs into different days of the week. Be orderly about prayer. All too often God has to say to us, "You do not have what you want because you do not ask God for it."[18]

Above all, ask God to fill you with his Holy Spirit. You have already received the Spirit into your life, if you have received Christ as your Lord and Savior. But pray that your whole life might now be filled with, or controlled by, the Spirit. This was the vital power of the early Church, and of every Christian since then, whose life has really counted for God. It is the Spirit who will reveal Jesus and make God increasingly real in your experience. It is the Spirit who will help you to understand the Bible, lead you out in prayer, help you to praise and worship God, and fill your heart with his love. It is the Spirit who can give you the strength and power to live for Jesus every day, and to speak for Jesus as the opportunities arise. "Be filled with the Spirit" is a command in the Scriptures,[19] and the tense of the verb means "go on being filled with the Spirit day by day." How?

In Luke 11:5-13 Jesus promised his disciples that his Father would certainly give the Spirit to those who ask him. The New Testament indicates that there are three important conditions which need to be fulfilled before this can happen. First, we must be willing to *repent*[20], or turn away, from any known sin, for the Spirit is the Holy Spirit and will not fill a vessel that wants to stay dirty. Second, we must be willing to *obey*[21] his leading in our lives; he wants to use us in God's service, not just to give us comforting or exciting spiritual experiences. Third, we must *hunger and thirst*[22] for God's best for our lives; the Spirit wants to know that we really mean business. If those conditions are fulfilled, Jesus told us not to doubt, but to "ask, and it will be given you; seek, and you will find; knock, and it will be opened to you." And he told us not to be afraid, for "what father among you, if his son asks for a fish, will instead of a fish give him a serpent; or if he asks for an egg, will give him a scorpion? If you then, who are evil know how to give good gifts to your children, how much more will the heavenly Father give the Holy Spirit to those who ask him!"[23]

3. *"What happens when I sin?"*

Sadly we all sin, often. But the answer is positive and clear: "If we confess our sins, [God] is faithful and just, and will forgive our sins and cleanse us from all unrighteousness."[24] When we receive Jesus we begin both a new relationship and a new friendship. The new relationship is fixed: I can never cease to be the son of my heavenly Father. But the new friendship, like all friendships, is much more delicate. We shall need often to say "sorry," to come back to Jesus, and to restore the friendship that we have damaged.

4. *"Can I keep it up?"*
Answer: No, not in your own strength. But God "is able to keep you from falling and to present you without blemish before the presence of his glory with rejoicing."[25] When I walk down the road with my little son we often go hand-in-hand. Sometimes he stumbles on a stone, but I am holding his hand firmly and he does not fall. Frequently we stumble in our Christian walk with Jesus. But his promise is clear: "They shall never perish, and no one shall snatch them out of my hand."[26] By the strengthening power of the Spirit of Jesus within us, we are enabled to do what we could never do on our own.

Do not be surprised if at times you face real problems in your new-found faith, perhaps especially the temptation to doubt: doubting the reality of your faith or even of God himself. Indeed you should be surprised if problems do not arise! At the baptism of Jesus his Father assured him, "You are my own dear Son. . . ." Shortly afterwards Jesus, in the wilderness, was severly tempted by Satan: "*If* you are God's Son. . . . *If* you are God's Son. . . ."[27] In the same way, you may face the same agonizing doubts shortly after you have received Jesus: "*If* you are a Christian, why don't you feel different? *If* Jesus is with you, why does he seem so far away?" Three times Jesus countered Satan by quoting Scripture. Learn a few promises from God, and this can help enormously when faced with doubts.

Other problems, too, may upset you at times: absence of feeling, the apathy or skepticism of the world, getting nothing from prayer or from the Bible, being let down or disappointed by other Christians, puzzling questions you cannot answer, sudden tragedy or bereavement, failure and defeat, the old desires still very active for a way of life you know is wrong. Remember, however, that you have entered into a *relationship,* and all relationships have problems from time to time. For example, don't worry about those feelings. I am not sure that I "feel" married at this moment (whatever that means) but I know that I am! Be open and honest with your problems. Talk to God about them, and, if possible, share them with an older, mature Christian friend. Paul once wrote: "Every temptation that has come your way is the kind that normally comes to people. For God keeps his promise, and he will not allow you to be tempted beyond your power; but at the time you are tempted he will give you the strength to endure it, and so provide you with a way out."[28]

My relationship with other Christians

Peter, using the building analogy says, "Come to him [Jesus], to that living stone, rejected by men but in God's sight chosen and precious: and like living stones be yourselves built into a spiritual house. . . ."[29]

If you saw some stones from a building lying in a heap on their own beside the building, it would be obvious that not only are they in the wrong place and useless, but the rest of the building would be considerably weakened by their absence. We, too, must be "like living stones" firmly in place with the rest of the "spiritual house". We cannot go it alone. We need active fellowship with other Christians. And, should we mistakenly think that *we* do not need the help of others, they certainly need our help. John Wesley once said, "Remember you cannot serve him alone; you must, therefore, find companions or make them; the Bible knows nothing of solitary religion." The Christians in New Testament days came at once into fellowship with other disciples of Christ.

Therefore get involved with your local church or Christian Union or Christian fellowship (whatever it may be called). Go along to the services on Sunday and to meetings for Bible study and prayer. Get to know others who know and love Jesus. In some churches that may not be altogether easy. The apostle Paul had a very difficult time when he tried to join up with other Christians after his conversion.[30] But he persevered because he knew it was important. Fellowship is one of God's ways of strengthening our faith; if we neglect this, we have only ourselves to blame for the problems that will certainly arise.

Of course, there are churches and churches! To begin with, at least, do your utmost to find one that is alive, that will give you good Bible teaching, that will help you to worship God and serve him. Link up with a small Bible study or prayer group as well, if you can, and welcome the help of a mature Christian for further guidance. With the right person this can be of the greatest help, as I found for the first few months of my Christian life. The more we get involved in Christian fellowship and service, the more the reality of Christ's presence will be experienced in our lives: "Where two or three are gathered in my name, there am I in the midst of them."[31]

My relationship with the world

"You are . . . a holy nation," wrote Peter, "God's own people, that you may declare the wonderful deeds of him who called you out of darkness into his marvellous light."[32] Two facts emerge from this statement.

First, as God's own people, we are called to be *holy*. There is nothing negative or killjoy about holiness. Its root meaning is to be "set apart": set apart, that is, from sin to God. We need to *show* others by our lives that God is real, that Jesus is alive, and that his Spirit can make, indeed has made, all these things true. Nothing is more important that the unconscious influence of a life impregnated with the Spirit of Jesus. A major reason for Christ's own magnetic attraction was that he manifestly loved everyone, however "worldly" or "sinful" they might have been, and yet he himself was different. Therefore they were puzzled and intrigued. Nothing is so powerful as a Christ-like life.

If we see ourselves as now set apart for Jesus, we must be careful about what we say and do. In practice, these three questions will nearly always guide you when you are not sure about a course of action:

1. Will it help or hinder my Christian life? (Hebrews 12:1f).
2. Will it help or hinder someone else's Christian life (1 Corinthians 8:9ff).
3. Is it to the glory of God? (1 Corinthians 10:31-11:1).

Or, summarizing these with one simple, searching

test: Can I really pray about it? These are some of the questions that we must ask carefully and honestly before God, all the time letting God's word in the Bible be our guide concerning our life and behavior.

Second, as God's own people, we are to *declare* his wonderful deeds, or to be witnesses to Jesus. The Christian faith is to be shared. God loves the whole world. Christ has died "for our sins, and not for ours only but also for the sins of the whole world."[33] It is a part of a Christian's responsibility and privilege to help others find Christ too. Your immediate responsibility is your own circle of friends and acquaintances. If you are not an effective "missionary"—and a missionary is simply someone "sent by God"—in that circle there is no other Christian in the world who can do that work for you. Learn as much as you can about the Christian faith, discovering how to answer some of the questions that are raised time and time again. Be very clear, especially, as to how you could guide another person in his search for God.

A simple framework might be as follows:

Something to *Admit:*	The fact of sin and the need for forgiveness: Romans 3:23; 6:23; Isaiah 59:2.
Something to *Believe:*	Christ has died to take away your sin: Isaiah 53:5-6; 1 Peter 2:24; 3:18.
Something to *Consider:*	Christ must come first in your life: Mark 8:34-38.

156

Something to *Do:*   Ask Christ into your life:
Revelation 3:20

Many are confused about the reality of God or their personal relationship with him. Therefore a logical sequence of steps, with verses, can be of the greatest help. However, we must never throw texts at people; but rather, with the sensitivity of love, seek to show them the truth about Jesus in whatever way we can. Above all, pray for the Spirit's guidance, remembering that God is searching for us long before we begin to search for him.

[1] Luke 19:5ff (J. B. Phillips)
[2] Psalm 95:7
[3] II Corinthians 6:2
[4] Isaiah 55:6
[5] Romans 6:23
[6] Mark 11:24
[7] For further reading, see *New Life, New Lifestyle* by Michael Green (Inter-Varsity), an excellent book full of practical help.
[8] 1 Peter 1:23, 25
[9] E.g. Revelation 3:20; John 6:37; John 10:28; Matthew 11:28-30
[10] See also Hebrews 10:19-23.
[11] See 1 John 2:3, 15, 29; 3:9, 14, 21; 5:4, 14
[12] Romans 8:15f
[13] 1 Peter 2:2f
[14] Such as those produced by the Scripture Union, 1716 Spruce St., Philadelphia, Pa., and the Navigators, P.O. Box 1659, Colorado Springs, Co. 80901.
[15] E.g., Psalms 1, 8, 23, 27, 32, 34, 40, 51, 84, 95, 96, 100, 103, 121, 139
[16] E.g., Philippians, 1 Thessalonians, 1 Peter
[17] For further reading: *Praying in the Spirit* by Arthur Wallis (Christian Literature Crusade), *Prayer* by O. Hallesby (Augsburg), *Prayer Without Pretending* by Anne Townsend (SU) HTTWG-(HSP).
[18] James 4:2 (TEV)
[19] Ephesians 5:18
[20] Acts 2:38
[21] Acts 5:32
[22] Matthew 5:6; John 7:37-39
[23] Luke 11:9, 11-13
[24] 1 John 1:9
[25] Jude 24
[26] John 10:28
[27] Luke 3:22; 4:1-13 (TEV)
[28] 1 Corinthians 10:13 (TEV)
[29] 1 Peter 2:4f
[30] Acts 9:26f
[31] Matthew 18:20
[32] 1 Peter 2:9
[33] 1 John 2:2